AUSTRALIA

steve *parish*: *the journey*

Steve Parish™

PUBLISHING

The joy is in the journey.

*Photography is like life's journey: repeating patterns forming stories,
which, when shared, have meaning for others who search as I do.*

*Exploring, discovering, hoping, wondering, dreaming, imagining –
all motivate my daily life. However, I have learnt that exercising my
mind this way is not enough to satisfy my spirit. More inspiring to
me is communicating, in words and images, the profound effect that
Nature has on my life. It is my hope that my observations, thoughts
and ideas will enhance other people's lives.*

So, sharing is the reason for my journey; it is my reason for being.

Opposite: *The great red rock, Uluru, physical symbol of this ancient land and spiritual symbol of its people.
This place has had a profound effect on my life – it stays with me.*

AUSTRALIA: THE JOURNEY

This mighty continent is made for adventuring; it is full of natural marvels and unique plants and animals. There are primeval rainforests, awesome deserts, rugged, snow-capped ranges and a coastline of scenic splendours. The Great Barrier Reef, with its teeming marine life and enchanting islands, extends some 2000 kilometres along the north-eastern coast, and on the other side of the country are the dolphins and dugongs of Shark Bay. It is not necessary to travel far from the major cities to encounter fantastic landforms such as the Twelve Apostles in Victoria or the Three Sisters in New South Wales. Longer, well-planned adventures are safe and rewarding. A few hours' drive takes travellers from Darwin to Kakadu; a few hours in a plane brings the majestic sight of Uluru, that awe-inspiring rock in the centre of the continent.

Australia's cities are safe places to stroll, to savour the sights and to enjoy great meals and sophisticated shopping and entertainment. Country towns offer their own delights, from warm hospitality to historic buildings and a taste of life on the land outback. This is my Australia, and I spend as much time as I can journeying its highways and byways, always finding new places to see and new sights to record on film.

Creating this book has been a journey in itself. It has taken me three years to complete, although the images span three decades and the stories have collected over my lifetime. During its compilation I relived the ecstasy of wild encounters, the adventure of new places, the joy of sharing and the dread of failure when confronting enormous challenges.

The huge task of structuring the images and experiences into a book was simplified by editing them into Australia's broad climatic areas of tropical, arid and temperate lands, coasts and seas. Then, while I was browsing the enormous library of images I have collected, memories of journeys flooded back and I created short word and photo essays reflecting the meaning and beauty of my experience. Each topic, whether hunting for orchids, stalking fish for close-up portraits or wandering urban streets in search of the character of a city, is an intrinsic part of my fascination for documenting Australia. My wild orchid pursuit is a recent obsession; others, such as fish photography, go back to my childhood when the stunning pictures in the pages of *National Geographic* kindled my forty-year love affair with fish.

My objective in this book is to communicate the sense of wonder and personal empowerment that is Nature's gift, a gift that has blessed me throughout my life. I would like this book to instil in you a desire to record your own journey, whether in words or pictures made with a computer, pen, brush, needle and yarn or, my choice, a camera. I strongly believe that through sharing our feelings, stories, hopes and dreams, we are nourished and grow. Nature, too, is our responsibility and requires care; but my worry is, if we do not care for each other and ourselves, how can we possibly care for the environment that sustains us?

This is a special book I created to share with you some of the places, people and events from my life; the journeys within the journey that have shaped me into the person I am today. So, I present some of the experiences of a lifetime: my journey.

Steve Parish

Opposite: *Reflected in the calm waters of a tropical billabong, a Jacana begins another journey.*

THE JOURNEYS

Left: *Journeying the Flinders Ranges, South Australia.*

TEMPERATE JOURNEYS

FROM THE EASTERN SEA-CLIFFS TO THE WESTERN HEATHLANDS

Many of our finest national parks are established within the temperate area of Australia. Some, such as the Blue Mountains, the Alpine, Wilson's Promontory, the Grampians, Southwest and Flinders Chase National Parks, are relatively large in area, others a mere pinprick on the map. Each wild area of the temperate belt is different from the next, and the whole area is of enormous interest to anyone fascinated by the natural world, and particularly anyone hooked on the excitement of photography.

Until I was thirty, when I moved to the subtropical city of Brisbane, I lived in many of the major cities and explored their coasts in detail. My early photography was solely focused on the underwater fringes of this vast island. It was not until 1981 that I emerged from the deep and turned my attention to *terra firma* and its multitude of facets. My early intention was to tell the story of Australia's fauna and its relationship to the natural environment. As time passed my interest widened to include plants, then the built environment, people and the Australian way of life. Today, I find this broad approach challenging, and with this outlook I am developing a deeper understanding of and passion for the Australian story.

Most Australians live, play and work in the warm and cool temperate areas of the southern states. Within this sweeping arc of land lie the capital cities of Sydney, Melbourne, Hobart, Adelaide, Perth and the nation's capital, Canberra. This part of Australia is the most highly developed. But, when you consider that, with a population of only about 14 million, it is about eight times the area of the United Kingdom (population 60 million) or about a sixth of the United States (population 280 million), the term "highly developed" is obviously relative.

Temperate Australia, containing the majority of our industrial centres, rolling green farmlands and many hamlets, towns and cities, offers alluring and interesting photographic challenges.

Previous pages: *Temperate seas lap temperate shores (South East Point, Wilsons Promontory National Park, Victoria).*

Opposite: *Crystal waters cascade through cool temperate forest (Liffey Falls, Tasmania).*

MELBOURNE – CITY OF GARDENS

Melbourne is Australia's second-largest city, a cosmopolitan metropolis that lives up to its motto, "We gather strength as we grow". In the city centre, gracious nineteenth-century buildings stand beside glass-sheathed commercial towers, symbolising the coexistence of Melbourne's colonial traditions with its vigorous modern lifestyle. Twenty-first-century Melbourne, on the banks of the Yarra River, is one of the great cities of the world.

Melbourne is built on comparatively level ground, and its suburbs stretch for great distances. The city has a population of around three and a half million, yet it is noted for courtesy and friendliness – perhaps the many green spaces offer opportunities to relax from big-city stress. Melbourne is a great place to shop. It is also a cultured city, with theatre of various genres staged in numerous locales – including the open air – a lively music scene, and magnificent artistic venues in the Victorian Arts Centre and the National Gallery of Victoria. Something I love to do is just wander along the Yarra's banks, admiring the river and the views of the city skyline.

I spent the first five years of my life in Melbourne and my first contacts with nature were along the shores of Port Phillip Bay, so this is a special place for me.

Top: *One of the famous Melbourne trams passes the city's most distinctive landmark, Flinders Street Station.*
Right: *That magic dawn light on the Yarra as it meanders past the city and under Princes Bridge.*
Opposite page: *Melbourne from the air looking over the Shrine of Remembrance.*

CITY ON A BAY

The shoreline of Port Phillip Bay is sheltered from much of the turbulence of the open sea, and the Bay waters abound in marine life. With magnificent fishing, swimming and boating to be had, the bay suburbs nearest the city's heart provide water sports and seaside activities that include roller-blading, cycling, walking and jogging.

One of my favourite pastimes on a warm, sunny, summer day in Melbourne is to grab my telephoto lens and visit the seaside suburb of St Kilda. Strolling through Sunday street markets and walking the pier is a very Melbourne thing to do. At the end of St Kilda Pier there is a famous coffee shop, a good place to sit and people-watch, and, in the evening, visitors can see Little Penguins returning to their nests along the rocks of the breakwater. It is at these times, admiring the faces of many cultures, that I am on the lookout for a quirky character or two for my lens.

Opposite page: *Melbourne through the forest of masts of boats moored at St Kilda.*
Left: *Melburnians strolling along St Kilda Pier.*

FOOTSTEPS TO THE SEA

My first memorable contact with the natural world was on the sandy beaches of Port Phillip Bay in Victoria. Between the ages of three and five, I visited the Bay with my family on bright, sunny weekends, and it was here that I first became utterly fascinated by the sea.

With the hot sun on my back, sand between my toes, water lapping around my legs, I experienced that delicious sucking, sinking feeling of the backwash of the waves. Then the journey home – all hot and sticky, sand everywhere and hair stiff with salt, and that wonderful tiredness, lulled into sleep by warmth and the drumming of tyres on bitumen.

These formative moments, so vivid in my memory, must surely have influenced the direction I would take later in life in becoming a diver.

Left: *The bathing boxes on Brighton Beach are a Melbourne landmark.*

TIME AND AGAIN

The Twelve Apostles are a major landscape signature of Victoria and, each time I travel the world-famous Great Ocean Road, I pause to reshoot the wondrous sunsets. Contemplating the valiant limestone stacks, I reflect on what has happened in my life since the last visit.

And, each time that I am there, the sun, sky and sea are in different moods, challenging me to make new images that capture this dramatically wild place. For me, going to this wave-tossed shore will never be a case of "been there, done that".

Above: The renowned Twelve Apostles in three of their many moods, all of which have fascinated me over the last fifteen years.

ADELAIDE – CITY OF MEMORIES

South Australia's capital, Adelaide, has long been a centre of cultural life. It is also one of the world's best laid-out cities, surrounded by parklands, graced with many elegant buildings and the winding charms of the River Torrens. North of Adelaide are the scenic splendours of the Flinders Ranges; to the east the Murray River flows through the Murraylands to the bird-haunted wilderness of the Coorong; to the south is the fertile Fleurieu Peninsula and Kangaroo Island; and to the west is a sea coast whose unspoiled beauty is equalled by its rich marine life.

Much of the State is arid country, but the fertile lands surrounding Adelaide produce wines to vie with the world's best and a smorgasbord of fine produce. South Australia also yields mineral wealth and opals. From the depths of the Blue Lake to the salt pans of Lake Eyre, South Australia is a State of exciting contrasts.

Adelaide stands on Gulf St Vincent and is sheltered to the east by the Mount Lofty Ranges. Surveyor-General Light's plan imposed a grid of streets around five squares, surrounded by extensive parklands. This and the glorious Mediterranean climate make Adelaide a tourist's dream in which landmarks are easy to find and there are plenty of green spaces for relaxation. An early influx of European settlers and continuing migration have fostered Adelaide's multiculturalism. The city hosts an internationally famous Festival of Arts, the largest of its kind in the southern hemisphere.

As part of my many journeys around Australia I love to visit Adelaide, where I lived between the ages of five and eighteen. I stare at my old school, the houses we called "home", and walk the streets of my childhood, particularly Port Adelaide, which contributed to my early love of ships and the sea. Adelaide is my memory lane.

Top right: *Port Adelaide Lighthouse and docks fascinated me as a child.*

Bottom right: *On the Glenelg foreshore lies the anchor of the sailing ship* Trottman, *discovered off Glenelg and presented as a bicentennial gift in 1988.*

Opposite page: *Looking south-east over Adelaide city towards the Mount Lofty Ranges.*

SIMPLY REMARKABLE

The site of my very first overnight camping experience in the bush was Cape du Couedic in the south-west of Flinders Chase National Park on Kangaroo Island. In stormy weather this is a spectacular place to sit and stare. Admiral's Arch is the Cape's primary landscape feature and a few kilometres away at Kirkpatrick Point lies what I consider to be one of Australia's most dramatic natural sculptures.

Blasted by wind and rain over aeons of time, Remarkable Rocks sit for all the world as though loving artistic hands had placed them there. This wild place is a must to visit, particularly at dawn and dusk when the oblique golden rays of the sun enhance shadows and colour.

Behind the steep seacliffs is heathland best experienced in spring when hundreds of flowers explode in a spectacle of colour and sweet aroma.

Right: *Admiral's Arch, a great place to watch the sun set.*
Opposite page: *Remarkable Rocks, sculpted by Nature.*
Both in Flinders Chase National Park, Kangaroo Island, South Australia.

FIRST CITY – FIRST IMPRESSIONS

Sydney, capital of New South Wales, radiates from the shores of Sydney Harbour. Internationally recognised as one of the world's great cities, it has a population of about four million people. It has come a long way since the Union Jack was raised on the shores of Sydney Cove on the 26th of January, 1788.

Today, this sparkling, energetic, exciting city is the first port of call for many – it is Australia's most visited tourist destination. The breathtaking Opera House and Harbour Bridge have become national icons, rivalled only by Red Kangaroos, Uluru and Koalas.

The Harbour and its foreshore have special significance for me. As a young sailor, I lived in Sydney from 1964 to 1969, on ships large and small, and in Mosman, Rushcutters Bay, Rose Bay and Watsons Bay – places that today boast some of Australia's most expensive real estate. In those days, the Harbour was my whole focus: I sailed over, swam under and honed my diving skills at bases around this glorious stretch of water.

Left: *Sydney, looking south-west from Point Piper.*

Above: *First impressions of the busy seaport of Sydney are created daily.*

Following pages: *World-famous symbols of Australia – the Harbour Bridge and Opera House.*

LIFE'S A BEACH

For many Australians life is indeed a beach. The golden beaches of the warm tropics are justly famous, but temperate Australia is bounded by long, sweeping beaches and small, intimate sandy coves. Some of the best surf in the country, and therefore the world, rolls in to temperate Australian beaches right around the coasts from west to east.

More than two-thirds of the 14 million people in Australia's temperate regions live within easy reach of the world's best beaches. For many, the relationship with the sun, sand and sea is almost a religious experience, providing relief from the heat of summer and release from the stresses of modern lifestyles. Beaches are places for meeting, relaxing, fishing, surfing, exercising, dreaming, and just being.

Opposite page: *Bondi Beach, perhaps the best-known beach in Australia.*
Left, top and bottom: *Surfers, swimmers and sun worshippers love Australian surf beaches from the east right round to the west.*

A FAVOURITE WILD ISLAND

My favourite wild Australian island is in the south Pacific Ocean, 700 km east and a bit north of Sydney. Lord Howe Island is small and breathtakingly beautiful, just 11 km long and 2.8 km at its widest point. Included on the UNESCO World Heritage List in 1982, the island is bordered by a reef-fringed lagoon, rolling surf, and the world's southernmost coral reefs. Lord Howe Island has few more than 350 residents, a sleepy village and moderate tourist infrastructure.

The ruggedly spectacular volcanic peaks of Mount Gower and Mount Lidgbird dominate the landscape, and about 75% of the island and its islets are preserved as permanent park. The islands boast a wide variety of plant and animal species, including large colonies of nesting seabirds and the native woodhen, a charming little flightless bird saved from near-extinction by a controlled breeding program.

The diving is spectacular, and the marine life is a combination of cool and warm temperate, and subtropical and tropical. The warm currents from the northern Coral Sea support fine corals, which encourage a rich fish life. It is paradise for walkers, birdwatchers and anglers – deep sea, beach and rock fishing are all popular, as are golf, tennis, bowling, cycling, surfing, snorkelling and scuba diving.

Top: *Balls Pyramid, Lord Howe Island.*

Right: *Lord Howe Island, one of Nature's finest gifts.*

ECSTASY IN THE BLACK

For most people, "the black" refers to a bank statement that is positive. To me, it is the deep water off southern New South Wales, a world that extends from 30 to 50 m beneath the surface. Even on a sunny day, little light penetrates this zone. Hundreds of times I have entered the black struggling with a camera in a cumbersome underwater housing and a hand-held torch.

Between 1969 and 1974, diving the black obsessed me; it demanded a considerable amount of physical skill, a great deal of training and self-discipline. I was driven to take care by the realisation that a diver who ignored the dangers of the deep did not survive to gloat over pictures taken there. Too long in deep water may cause the fatal diving sickness known as "the bends".

Whilst diving, my adrenaline levels rose with apprehension but simultaneously I felt excited anticipation. The black was filled with twisted corals, bizarre sponges, big-eyed cuttles, multitudes of molluscs, and enough fish of all shapes, sizes, and colours to fill a young photographer's heart with joy. At this time many species photographed were new to science and most images taken were firsts, a fascinating thought for a curious, young, diving photographer.

Right: *Seawhip Anemones were new to science when I first photographed them in 1969 in 40 m of water off Jervis Bay, New South Wales.*
Opposite page, left to right: *The surface of a deep-sea sponge; the precise patterns of the Vermilion Biscuit Seastar; a macro of the surface of a Fire-brick Seastar. An underwater flash is essential to bring out the living colours of these deep-water animals.*

A FISHY OBSESSION

A youthful passion for shooting rabbits developed my stalking skills. Equipped with a telescopic sight and a silencer (illegal today), I would lie in wait at rabbit warrens for hours, attempting to bag as many furry pests as possible for the table.

Later, armed with a spear gun, I was as skilled when hunting fish. But I didn't find dead fish very interesting, and, given a camera to work with, I became irretrievably lost in a new world of fish and their fascinating behaviour.

On my early photographic expeditions, I thought it would be easy to transfer my hunting skills … and was not entirely wrong. I am not talking about stalking a fish to within a metre or two, but stalking it to within centimetres. Fish are far from stupid – their lives depend on a daily, lifelong, deadly game of hide and seek with both predator and prey alike. To outwit a fish and achieve an in-focus photograph requires far more talent than to kill it.

Right, top to bottom: A blue-tipped Long-fin in a courting display; unique Pineapplefish that employ tiny headlights under their jaw to find their prey; a colourful Banded Seaperch.
Opposite page: A Butterfly Gurnard creeps across the seafloor on pectoral rays.

CANBERRA – THE NATION'S CAPITAL

Surrounded by New South Wales, the Australian Capital Territory is the setting for the nation's capital city, Canberra, in the beautiful valley of the Molonglo River, which was dammed to form Lake Burley Griffin. More than half of the ACT is set aside for parks and reserves, including Namadgi National Park. The ACT offers the full gamut, from sophisticated city life to experiences of pristine bushland wilderness and fascinating wildlife.

About halfway between Sydney and Melbourne, Canberra is an easy few hours by road from either. Founded in 1913, it was designed to be the home of Australia's federal institutions and diplomatic missions from abroad. Multicultural and hospitable, Canberra is a place where people can explore Australia's past, present and future in a lovely city planned to reflect the national spirit.

Spacious and magnificently endowed with gardens, the national capital puts on its party clothes in March, when the ten-day Canberra Festival attracts more than 200 000 visitors to celebrate its founding. Brilliant autumn leaves form a blazing backdrop to concerts, a street parade and the fireworks of Skyfire. Trademarks of this birthday party are the multicoloured hot-air balloons that soar from the Parliamentary foreshore and carry their enthralled passengers over the city.

The other great festival is in springtime, when Floriade fills Commonwealth Park with floral splendour and crowds enjoy the city's private and public gardens and a host of cultural events. Spring is also the time of year to experience many of the nation's most spectacular wildflowers at the Australian National Botanic Gardens.

Right, top to bottom: Canberra from the lookout at Mount Ainslie; a hot-air balloon over the National Museum; Canberra from the air; the spectacular National Botanic Gardens.
Opposite page: Michael Nelson Jagamara, a renowned artist from Papunya in Central Australia, designed the mosaic in the Parliament House forecourt. The design embodies the coming together of ancestors to enact ceremonial "business".

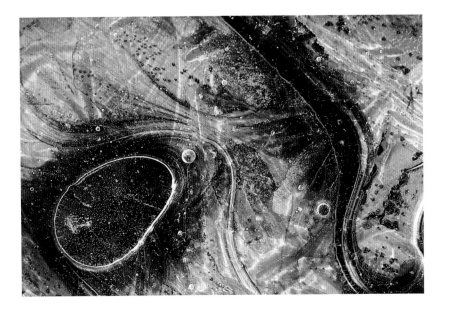

THE AUSTRALIAN ALPS

The magnificent alpine country of south-eastern New South Wales was a well-kept secret for many years before the Snowy Mountains scheme constructed a system of roads, tunnels, dams and power stations to provide hydro-electric power and irrigation reservoirs. Suddenly access to the high country in both winter and summer became easy, and the fame of Australia's Alps spread worldwide. Today Kosciuszko National Park stretches along the Great Divide from the Australian Capital Territory to the Victorian border. It contains Mount Kosciuszko, the highest mountain in Australia (2228 m), a group of excellent ski resorts and vast stretches of rugged wilderness rich in mountains, lakes and exceptional wildlife. The snow-white world of the winter months is indeed a photographic paradise.

Above: *Ice art in the Australian Alps.*
Right: *The spectacular Snow Gum, which, in the golden glow of early morning or late afternoon light, creates a stunning effect against the snow-country landscape.*
Opposite page: *Kosciuszko National Park, New South Wales.*

TASMANIA – TRULY BLESSED BY NATURE

Ninth-largest and second-oldest city in Australia (it was founded in 1804), Hobart, capital of Tasmania, has a population of nearly 200 000. Built on the banks of the Derwent River with Mount Wellington as backdrop, Hobart is a beautiful gem of a city, whose people prize their buildings dating from the colonial and convict era. The superb harbour is important to the city's commercial life, and is the goal for competitors in the deepwater Sydney to Hobart Yacht Race.

The wilderness is so close to Hobart! The city is a gateway to unequalled wild places, from long beaches and coastal lagoons to towering stone peaks, rushing rivers and seemingly endless forests and windswept upland plateaus.

When I'm in Hobart, I love to visit the Saturday markets at Salamanca Place. In a world of bartering and bantering, there are always people promoting political issues and opinions of the day. Whether or not I agree with the opinions being voiced, it is a great democratic experience.

Opposite page: *Hobart, the capital of Tasmania.*
Left: *The Saturday markets at Salamanca Place.*
Above: *Vessels of the fishing fleet at Constitution Dock.*

HIDE AND SEEK

While wandering northern Tasmania, recovering from a severe bout of flu, I was lured by a rare sunny day into the cool waters of Bass Strait. The marine world in this area has an eeriness – fronds of giant kelp may grow 45 m from the ocean floor up to the surface.

On entering the water I was joined, amongst the swaying kelp, by a group of young fur-seals, their big black eyes and quivering whiskers expressing their joyful determination to play with me.

From the surface a seal would barrel-roll down at me, its apparent aim to score a direct hit on my head. When collision seemed inevitable, the sleek missile would come to a dead stop just centimetres from my facemask. The halt was absolute, without the flipper-waving follow-through one would expect in this watery world.

Then, to top off the display, the seal would blow bubbles, pirouette, and, with its head doubling back over its rump, dash for the kelp. After hiding briefly, it would peer back as though inviting me to join the game. Alas, that I were nimble enough!

Right: *Young fur-seals play hide and seek.*

Opposite page: *Wineglass Bay, Freycinet National Park – its wild beauty defies description.*

GREENER PASTURES

Australians have long had a love affair with things old, but during the past two years I've noticed a real surge in the restoration of heritage buildings. There are more gift shops specialising in memorabilia and antiques, and there's more community art depicting scenes from Australia's past. At times, this passion for the past conflicts with a vision for the future, for example, where restorers and developers have different ideas about the best use of space and the value of existing structures.

So what's all the fuss about? Why are we so intent on preserving and restoring? Restoration is certainly good for the soul. Nostalgia has a certain sad sweetness. Perhaps this fascination is due to a longing to return to a simpler, less complex life, a time when the grass appears greener. But perhaps it can be attributed to a growing national maturity and appreciation of our past and its effect on our place in the modern world.

Pastures are greener, to me, when they are nurtured with an eye to our heritage as well as to our present needs and our aspirations.

Left: *Absolute contentment in Stanley, Tasmania — what more could a cow wish for?*
Above: *A picture-postcard cottage in Richmond, Tasmania.*

PERTH – A CITY IN THE SUN

Basking on the banks of the broad Swan River in the relatively warm winters and hot summers of a Mediterranean climate, Perth, the capital of Western Australia, is a memorable place to visit. Perth and its sister-port, Fremantle, are more than 2000 km distant from Adelaide. Their residents are remarkably self-sufficient in matters of art, cuisine and culture: the depth of local talent is showcased in the Festival of Perth held each February–March. Its population of more than 1.2 million people treasures the relaxed Perth lifestyle.

The Swan River curves through the centre of Perth. An efficient public transport system gives access to parks, playing fields, and walking and cycling tracks that border the river. Families swim at the sandy beaches, and picnic or barbecue in parklands shaded by spreading gums and peppermint trees. There are also some great fishing spots along the Swan. Any visit to the city should include a stroll around the lakes at the Narrows Interchange and a voyage upon the river's blue expanse. Nearby, the historic port of Fremantle is the access point for the popular holiday island of Rottnest.

Opposite page: *Perth, the capital of Western Australia, as seen from the air.*
Left, top to bottom: *Rottnest Island, a popular island just off the coast of Perth; Fremantle, the port city of Perth; Scarborough Beach, a popular city beach washed by the Indian Ocean.*

WILD AUSTRALIA IN SUBURBIA

Over the past few decades, there has been a strengthening interest in Australia's spectacular native plants, particularly for home cultivation. And why not? Australia, without doubt, has the most extraordinary array of wildflowers found anywhere in the world.

In Perth, the locals are exposed to the magnificent variety of wildflowers in the west and south-west of their state. In Kings Park in spring, it is possible to wander among flowers that I guarantee will stop you in your tracks.

When I first introduced native plants to my garden, I discovered, to my surprise, I had also brought birds to my home. My space was transformed into a different world, with colourful activity exploding before my eyes. Wildflower photography is currently my favourite form of creative relaxation. Getting close to flowers gives me considerable joy and I always wait eagerly for the return of the processed film.

I often joke that when I retire I will settle in the south-west of Western Australia. Maybe some sleepy town the world forgot such as Augusta, or Windy Harbour, in an area where I can enjoy the most beautiful wildflowers found anywhere in the world. The joke, of course, lies in the word "retire".

Opposite page: *The city of Perth from the native bush gardens of Kings Park.*
Top left: *A mannequin adorned with wildflowers, a feature of the Wildflower Festival held in spring in Kings Park, Perth.*
Bottom left, left to right: *Wildflowers and wildlife all enhance the quality of our lives, particularly when introduced to our own gardens.*

Top: *Flame pea* Bottom, left to right: *Geraldton Wax; Cranbrook Bell; Mountain Grevillea; Scarlet Banksia; Basket Flower; Pink Everlasting Daisy.*

Top: *Lilac Hibiscus* Bottom, left to right: *Pink Rainbow Sundew; Rose Coneflower; Yellow Lechenaultia; Red and Green Kangaroo Paw; Many-flowered Fringe Lily; Pink Rice Flower.*

THE TREASURE HUNT

Of all the bushland treasures, orchids are among the most sensational in terms of colour, form, shape and texture. Those shown here are all from the south-west of Australia where more than 300 of Australia's 1000 orchid species live. During their predominant flowering season, between September and November, little can rival the joy of hunting these botanical wonders.

To really appreciate their beauty, one has to get "up close and personal", on all fours. Sometimes, when I am down in the dirt with these delights, I find other delicacies for my lens – other flowers, insects and, on one occasion, a perfectly camouflaged skink that was well hidden from my eye when I was looking from six feet above the ground.

Opposite page, clockwise from far left: *Purple-veined Spider Orchid; Lazy Spider Orchid; Narrow-lipped Dragon Orchid; Pink Fairy; Custard Orchid; Dark-tipped Spider Orchid; Fringed Mantis Orchid. Clockwise from top left: White Spider Orchid; Queen of Sheba; Cowslip Orchid.*

SOUTH-WEST OBSESSIONS

Where pristine white sandy beaches are lapped by the aqua blue waters of the warm Indian Ocean, it is understandable that the sea features in favourite relaxation pursuits for the folk in south-west Western Australia. From Rottnest Island, just off the coast from Perth, down past Fremantle, around Cape Leeuwin, past Albany to Esperance, this is a very spectacular area, boasting some wonderful surfing, boating, fishing and wild coastal exploration opportunities.

Three fast-growing industries in the south-west are wineries, wildflower farming and arts and crafts, each going hand-in-glove with the other. Historically, the area was cleared for farming and, in the unique Jarrah and Karri forests, logging has long been practised. On each return, every three years or so, I find attitudes improving as more environmentally aware people move into the area.

Opposite page: *The Salmon Holes, Tornidirrup National Park near Albany, Western Australia.*
Above, clockwise from top left: *Spring blooms on the heathland; Cape Leeuwin; Karri forest; Sugarloaf Rock.*
All in Leeuwin–Naturaliste National Park, Western Australia.

TIDE-LINING

A long, lonely, sweeping beach is the most spectacular place to be, whether you are a photographer in search of magic, or someone with a passion for solitude.

Tide-lining gives me solace and is a great source of creative stimulation. I have conceived and indeed resolved many a challenging creative problem wandering along the edge of the water, enclosed in my own meditative capsule. Even in the crowds on a popular beach, I am able to create my own space.

On a lonely beach in the north-west or on the wilderness shores of Cape York Peninsula there are photo subjects just waiting to be discovered. Minutes have a habit of turning to hours, and days to weeks, in these wild places. There are footprints to make, mysteries to unravel, feathers, shells and strange sea plants to discover, then lightly made tracks to follow.

Above, left to right: *A cuttle bone at the tide's edge; raindrops on a feather on the beach magnify encapsulated sand; shell with wind-blown sand patterns.*
Opposite page: *A solitary tide-liner at William Bay National Park, Western Australia.*

THE HERITAGE TRAIL

During 2000 and 2001, I travelled more than 100 000 km around Australia. In that time I visited many regional towns and all of the major cities. I always "sweep" the back streets looking for character that lends itself to being photographed.

Over the years I have developed a broad interest in heritage buildings of all kinds. They've been around long enough to acquire character – some are aristocrats and some are larrikins. Tasmania is rich in heritage architecture, domestic and public, in so many places, such as Stanley, Sheffield, Launceston, Richmond and Hobart.

Some of the buildings and cottages have been so lovingly restored and maintained that they are a joy to this photographer's eye.

Opposite page: *The delightful historical seaport of Stanley, north-western Tasmania, is the birthplace of Joseph Lyons, Prime Minister of Australia, 1932–39.*
Left: *A wagon, cottage and grinding wheel – other images of Stanley, a perfect place to slip back in time.*

OBJECTS TO DELIGHT

Oil lamps of every imaginable size and shape, brass and porcelain statuettes, intricately painted tin boxes, cute little sailboats, finely etched jewellery, little dinner bells, cutlery in felt-lined hand-crafted wooden boxes … name it and you can find it in one of hundreds of antique and heritage shops, stores so full that browsing can take hours.

During my explorations I find myself wondering where on earth all this "stuff" originated. Talk to the shopkeepers and you soon find out that in the background there are folk who are obsessed with hunting out objects from our past. They wander the country investigating abandoned homes that have often been locked away by their inheritors for many years, combing through the stock in charity shops, bidding at auction, savouring the hunt and always looking for that unsuspected treasure.

Opposite page: *Treasures at Evandale, one of many Tasmanian towns on the heritage trail.*
Left: *An old homestead and shed in Western Australia. Such abandoned buildings are often the first port of call for treasure hunters searching for historical memorabilia.*

Left: *A beautifully restored Ford carries wine barrels from Hillstowe Wines in historic Hahndorf, South Australia.*

Right: Emmylou *takes heritage enthusiasts on daily cruises along the River Murray at Echuca, Victoria.*

Opposite page: *Puffing Billy carries steam train enthusiasts in the Dandenong Ranges, Victoria.*

Top: *The interior of an old-time corner shop painted on the external wall of a store at Streaky Bay, South Australia.*

Above: *Nineteenth-century life recreated on a water-tank near New Norcia, Western Australia.*

A work of art on a backyard shed in Sheffield, northern Tasmania.

Top: *A mural depicting life at the turn of the twentieth century on a shop wall in Peterborough, South Australia.*

Above: *A country road on a wall painting in northern Tasmania.*

THE THIN GREEN LINE

The first Australian legislation to protect scenic areas was passed in Tasmania: the *Waste Lands Act* of 1863. Australia's first national park, declared in 1879, was Royal National Park, south of Sydney. It was also the second national park in the world.

Today there are about 3200 protected areas in Australia, totalling more than 40 000 000 ha, about 5% of the continent. More than 200 marine and estuarine areas comprising 38 000 000 ha have also been reserved, and there is still considerable work to be done with marine conservation.

Many Australian national parks and reserves are within easy reach of main cities and towns and many parks contain evidence of Aboriginal culture – paintings, and ceremonial and sacred sites. These sites are protected and some are owned and managed by their indigenous custodians.

Every year, millions of people visit Australia's national parks, many of which have good walking tracks and picnic and camping grounds. It is always wise to check the conditions of entry with parks and reserves authorities before visiting.

While it may seem that Australia is well served by parks and reserves, I believe that 5% is very meagre when you consider the size of Australia. Conservation groups and environmental authorities are continually lobbying for additional protective legislation, and there still remains valuable representative habitat that is unprotected, habitat that supports some of the world's endangered plants and animals, many of which are found nowhere else on earth.

Left: *Russell Falls, Mount Field National Park, Tasmania.*

ISLANDS LOCKED IN TIME

Much of Australia's land mass has been cleared for agriculture and grazing. However, there are regions that have been locked away as conservation areas. Sometimes the existence of these wilderness "islands" is due to local foresight, but all too often they were left untouched because the clearing equipment of the day was unable to deal with the terrain or the land was considered unproductive.

These isolated areas can become havens for wildlife, particularly birds and mammals. An example is the Stirling Range National Park in south-west Western Australia: there are many other examples right across Australia. Stirling Range National Park, completely surrounded by cleared grazing land, is now considered to be one of the richest areas, botanically, in the world. In these artificial refuges, wildlife populations may increase, giving the false impression that animals exist in similar density throughout the wild world.

In some cases, such as Hattah-Kulkyne National Park in north-western Victoria, the habitat sanctuary the park offers resulted in a population explosion of Western Grey Kangaroos. In time the kangaroos became a major threat to surrounding agricultural lands, and they also threaten their own existence by over-grazing the comparatively small area of remaining native woodland.

Another island example is the Blue Mountains National Park, now a World Heritage Area, bordered in the west by agricultural land and in the east by the sprawling city of Sydney. One of the biggest threats to the unique plants and animals is fire, which too often is a result of the park's proximity to urban development.

Top right: *The Three Sisters, a feature of the magnificent Blue Mountains near Sydney, New South Wales.*
Bottom right: *Wild areas throughout temperate Australia support the highest diversity of wildflowers in the world.*
Opposite page: *Stirling Range National Park, south-west Western Australia.*

SPIRIT FUEL

I think falling and running water offer the highest octane of all the "spirit fuels" in the natural world.

Standing, sitting or lying, even sleeping on a smooth, flat rock beside a waterfall or a gently running creek, can uplift the spirit. The crystal flow reaches down inside you and washes away your troubles.

A favourite waterfall can be revisited. It can be a place to remember what has happened since you were last there, or to look ahead and dream of how to reach those special goals you hope to achieve. Australia has many waterfalls – most of the State capitals are within easy reach of plunging, healing cascades.

Clockwise from top left: *Fitzroy Falls, Morton National Park, New South Wales; Crystal Shower Falls, Dorrigo National Park, New South Wales; Erskine Falls, Angahook-Lorne State Park, Victoria; MacKenzie Falls, Grampians National Park, Victoria.*

Opposite page: *A swift-running stream in the ancient rainforest near Marysville, Victoria.*

REFLECTING ON FORESTS

An environmental issue causing controversy over the past thirty years is the protection of our forested areas. Travelling Australia back and forth, particularly when flying at low level, I see little remaining of the original old growth forest. In parts of Australia – south- and north-eastern New South Wales, Tasmania, the south-west of Western Australia and tropical north Queensland – the struggle goes on between harvesters and those who would argue that remaining forests are essential for the survival of the human race.

Recently, I flew over the coastal forests of southern New South Wales and was stunned when our little plane passed over the wood chip plant at Eden. There, strewn across the landscape, were hundreds of trees, each waiting its turn to become woodchip. This will be exported to be turned into cardboard or paper, much of which is returned to Australia. Every time I open a cardboard box I am reminded of Australia's few remaining forests and our responsibility to minimise our consumption of packaging.

The environment can only be on the political agenda through people power, and there have been classic examples of this at work. One was the election of the Hawke Government in 1983, a direct result of the green vote. Australian and, indeed, international communities demanded a stop to the damming of the Franklin River in Tasmania. I am heartened by the fact that today's environmentally aware young people will take leadership in our political landscape, and I hope it is not too late.

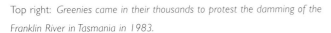

Top right: *Greenies came in their thousands to protest the damming of the Franklin River in Tasmania in 1983.*
Bottom right: *A woodchip site near Eden, New South Wales.*
Opposite page: *Classic old growth, cool temperate rainforest in Tasmania.*

BUSH MAGIC

To experience the magic of the Australian bush, it is worth getting up before dawn to watch the very first rays of sun paint the topmost leaves of the trees with light, then lay a wash downwards towards the dark understorey. The sight of mist covering the mountains, spilling down into the valleys, is simply beautiful.

Lizards crawl cautiously from hiding to bask in the life-giving warmth. Birds pause in their rapturous greeting of the new day, fluff their feathers and spread wings and tails like solar fans. Thumps and thuds betray kangaroos and wallabies returning to their daytime hideaways. Koalas wedge their furry bottoms into tree forks and prepare for another hard day's sleep. The sun rim-lights dewy grasses, and back-lights hanging gum leaves, revealing sap-filled veins in patterns as intricate as spider webs.

Australians love the bush: we love to know it is there offering an escape, and we love to spend time strolling, exploring, photographing, sitting, watching and listening. We picnic and barbecue, being careful not to spark a dreaded bushfire. Many Australians love the bush so much that they have chosen to build in bushland, taking quite a risk, as fires frequently sweep through, razing all in their path.

Above: *A Koala peers from its lofty perch in the Australian bush.*

Right: *Mist adds to the magic of this mountainous bushland in Tasmania.*

Opposite page: *In the morning light, river-fringing bushland reflects in the calm waters of the Denmark River, Western Australia.*

Following pages: *A gallery of bushland textures.*

ICONIC ANIMALS

In Australia, there are no herds of wildebeest being pursued by lions across savannah. We have no elephants or giraffes. What we have is far from obvious, often cryptic in colour and, if we talk about mammals, mostly active only at night. Why then are a number of our species international favourites?

In my observation, Australians are ardent fans of our own wildlife. I believe the primary reason is that many people are lucky enough to have wildlife in their own backyard. In urban Australia, where there are trees there are possums that rampage at night across the iron roof in their hob-nailed boots! And birds – parrots of all sorts, kookaburras, currawongs, butcher birds – and if they do not visit they can certainly be heard! In well-vegetated areas, there may be a mob of kangaroos resident close by. There are many areas of eastern Australia where Koala populations live in local parks, even in people's own back yards! Frogs chorus after rain has fallen, and geckos and lizards sun themselves on garden walls and fences.

So, I believe we are ardent fans of wildlife because we have a face-to-face relationship with our wild Australians. This is why I am a supporter of fauna parks and zoos – those that are well resourced and managed, of course. Without face-to-face time, no relationship can develop; without a relationship, no care for wild habitats will ensue. The motivation to conserve usually grows out of a reason, benefit or relationship.

Right and opposite page: *Popular wild Australians – the Koala and the Grey Kangaroo.*

Above, left to right: *The Common Wombat and the Short-beaked Echidna have stolen the hearts of many Australians.*

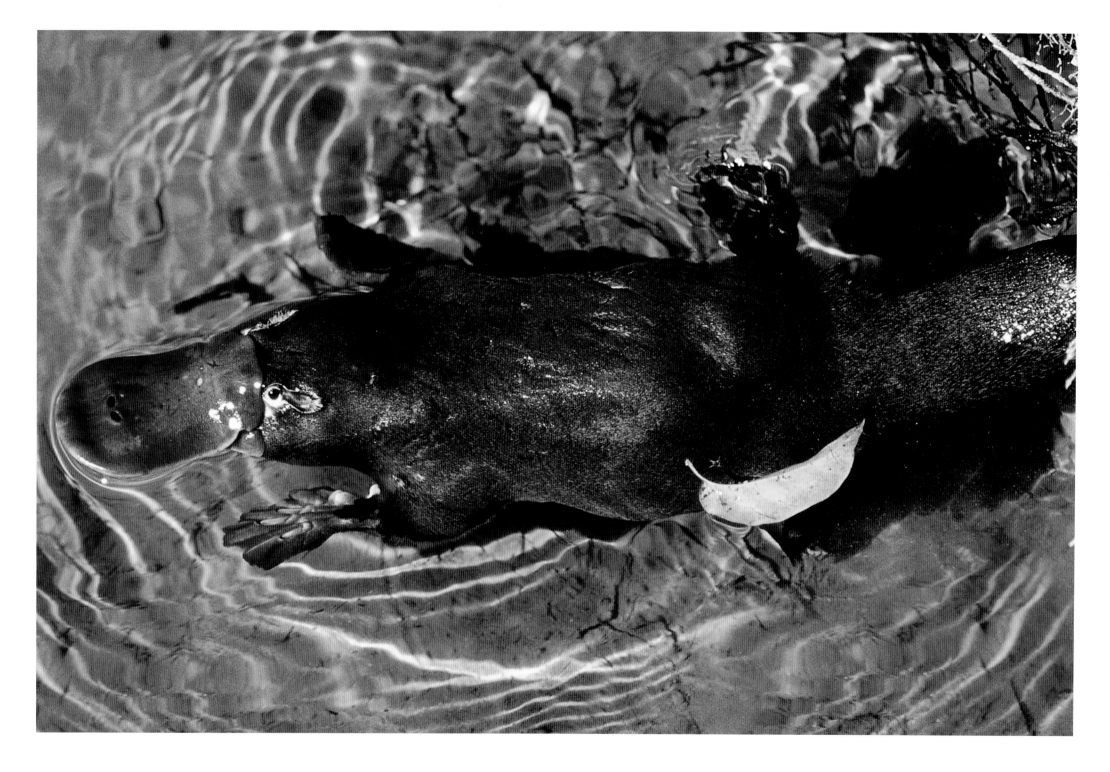

The Platypus prefers to hunt in crystal-clear streams far from the haunts of people.

Above, left to right: *The classic "eagle-eye" stare of the magnificent Wedge-tailed Eagle, Australia's largest bird of prey;*
the Laughing Kookaburra, a much-loved Australian bird whose raucous calls can be heard at dawn and dusk.

Above, left to right: *Major Mitchell's Cockatoo and the Sulphur-crested Cockatoo, two of Australia's avian icons.*

WHAT ABOUT US?

When I approached the Queensland National Parks Service in 1974 requesting employment as a wildlife photographer, I was asked, "... but have you photographed any land animals?" Volunteering to prove that I could, I set out for Lamington National Park's rainforest. At dark, after a day's hard walking, searching and snapping, I returned to Brisbane, hoping desperately that pictures of a fat brown spider and an even fatter black lizard would impress. They did not, but fortunately my dedication (or persistence) paid off and I was given the job on trial.

Under the guidance of wildlife experts, I soon learned where possums lived, met elusive quolls and bandicoots, discovered that most mammals do not keep office hours and that to photograph snakes needs nerves – and knees – of steel. My world for twenty years had been under water and I found this explosion of opportunity to learn about terrestrial wildlife absolutely thrilling.

I also learned that Australia's wildlife is highly susceptible to decline and extinction. While habitat alteration and eradication are the primary causes, the introduction of predatory mammals like cats and foxes has also contributed in an alarming way to both extinction and change of distribution for many small mammals.

Top right: *The Long-nosed Potoroo digs for food, playing a useful role in forest growth.*
Bottom right: *The Eastern Pygmy-possum is a mouse-sized possum that loves the nectar of flowering plants.*
Opposite: *A female Eastern Quoll, a cat-sized marsupial predator, with her young ones.*

ARID JOURNEYS

FROM GRASSY PLAINS TO WESTERN DESERT COASTS

There is something very special about the central aridlands of Australia that lures me back time and again. I love the red dunes draped in wildflowers, the rocky escarpments bespeckled with spinifex, the swaying golden grass on the plains, the waterholes and dry creeks lined with River Red Gums, the gibber plains and their sun-reflective stones. I sense the aeons in this ancient world, a land of red rock and blue sky, most spectacular when storm clouds from the west move in, overpowering the blue with towering castles of grey-black that flush vermilion as the sun sets.

Desert plants and animals fascinate me – in such dry country living things have adopted remarkable lifestyles simply to survive. Many, like the rare Southern Hairy-nosed Wombat of the inhospitable Nullarbor Plain, dig burrows that serve as refuges during the scorching day, then emerge to feed at night. At dawn on still days, the night's events are written on the dunes in the tracks of mammals, insects and reptiles.

Outback people are special: they too have adapted to this harsh environment, working and playing in places many urban Australians have never experienced. This is a world where friendship, trust and a helping hand still have meaning. Once welcomed into its mateship, it is hard to leave. Outstanding among the desert inhabitants are the indigenous people, who know the country in ways the rest of us struggle to understand. Part of the story of the land is told in traditional art shared with us by the Aboriginal peoples, and which is now sought by galleries around the world.

The arid heartlands of Australia stretch from western Queensland, New South Wales and Victoria clear across the top end of South Australia, through the lower half of the Northern Territory, to the coast of Western Australia. I remember all my journeys on the tracks, trails and highways of these arid lands, camping in dry creek beds on cold nights beneath inky black, star-filled skies and waking at dawn to a chorus of Galahs, corellas and crows. Photography refreshes these memories… not the heat, or the wind-blown sand in eyes and hair, or the flies in mouth and nose, but the red land, blue sky and silver-white of ghostly gums, so pale against shadowed purple ranges.

Left: *The rolling dunes of the Simpson Desert.*

THE PLACE CALLED ULURU

Uluru and Kata Tjuta symbolise Australia's desert heartland. To Anangu, the Aboriginal custodians of the park, this remarkable landscape is a record of the journeys and activities of ancestral beings who shaped the land and created life. Anangu, through a system of spiritual beliefs and cultural laws known as Tjukurpa, are responsible for the land's well-being and for its life forms.

The significance of the cultural, biological and geological features of Uluru–Kata Tjuta National Park is recognised internationally: it is both a World Heritage Area and a World Biosphere Reserve. Uluru, 348 m high and 9.4 km in circumference, is the tip of a great slab of sandstone thought to extend several kilometres under ground. Caves honeycomb its upper levels, gash its ribbed sides and undercut its base.

The Rock's near-vertical sides carry few plants, but thickets of bloodwood, wattle and fig cluster in gullies, waterholes and creek beds around the base. Sparse mulga, mallee, desert oaks and tussock grasses stabilise the sandplains and dunes.

Above and right: *The colour of Uluru changes as the day progresses, bringing different tones of red, orange and purple to the great rock.*

KATA TJUTA

About 30 km west of Uluru, the many-headed Kata Tjuta is a jumble of massive sandstone domes, narrow canyons and valleys. Mt Olga, 546 m above ground level, is the tallest of the 36 domes and also the highest point in the park.

Although there is no permanent water, the canyons and gorges retain rainwater for some time, and support a greater range of plants than Uluru, including River Red Gums and the delicate pink Early Nancy Lily.

As with Uluru, the changes of light bathe the Kata Tjuta massifs in wonderful colours. But just as impressive is the silence… a deep, awesome silence in which any sound, such as the call of an eagle, has wonderful clarity and purity of tone.

Kata Tjuta is a good wildlife-watching place. Many creatures are not readily seen during the heat of the day: they forage for food and water in the cooler evening and night, holing up in caves or burrows during the day. Some, like the Black-footed Rock-wallaby, are so well acclimatised that they have little need to drink water.

Above: *Kata Tjuta from the air.*
Right: *Glowing red in the warm light of the setting sun.*

Previous pages: *The Devil's Marbles, Devil's Marbles Conservation Park, Northern Territory.*

Opposite page: *A solitary grass-tree stands sentinel against the setting sun, Flinders Ranges, South Australia.*

Above, top to bottom: *Sunset glory – looking across Uluru towards Kata Tjuta; the MacDonnell Ranges; Kata Tjuta.*

THE BLOOMING DESERT

There are few sights more exquisite than a red desert landscape in full bloom following exceptional rains. In fact, helping people sink soul and senses into wildflower-scapes has become an industry, and pilgrims travel from all over the world to Australia's aridlands for the experience.

To stand in a field of blossoms stretching to the horizon is good for the spirit. It certainly diminishes a photographer's bank balance, as it is almost impossible to stop clicking away. On one journey, I arrived at Uluṟu after heavy rains. Not far from Yulara, a fantastic carpet of multi-coloured flowers was spread across the red sand. It was about a kilometre wide and ten long and its edges were clearly delineated, so the rain must have been very localised. Cars and tourist buses zoomed by, passengers staring ahead at the road, their sights and schedules set on reaching the next stop on their desert odyssey, oblivious to the rare display through which they were passing.

For a blooming good visit to Australia's arid wildernesses, I make the time to stop, look at and feel the colours, forms and textures of the red lands. Also, I call on local knowledge, study weather charts, and hope for lots of good luck.

Opposite page, top and bottom: *Wildflowers carpet the plains in Mount Augustus National Park, WA. Mount Augustus is Australia's largest monolith, larger than Uluṟu.*

Left: *After rain at Uluṟu, the sombre hues of the desert burst into colour.*

Above, left to right: *Desert Rose, floral emblem of the NT; Sturt's Desert Pea, floral emblem of SA.*

The dunes around Uluṟu after seasonal spring rains.

Poached Egg Daisies during a spring bloom at Rainbow Valley Conservation Reserve, Northern Territory.

DREAMING OF DINOSAURS

Australia is world-renowned for the quality of its fossil finds. The ancient rivers, floodplains, escarpments and ranges of outback Queensland are amongst the oldest on earth. When I'm sitting in the the cool shade of a gorge's towering cliffs in the stillness of a winter's day, I find it easy to imagine a dinosaur or two coming in from the plains to drink. In my mind's eye, I see their swaying, swishing tails and their hides glistening in the sun. I hear their heavy breathing and the thump of their huge feet. Indeed, this is the land of the dinosaurs, a landscape steeped in antiquity.

The area enclosed by Winton, Hughenden and Cloncurry has become known as the "fossil triangle". This is no longer drive-by territory because most of the towns have established interpretive museums, meticulous in their presentations.

This area was part of a shallow inland sea around 115 million years ago, hence most of the fossil remains are found in soft limestone from which it is easier to free the fossils than from the hard stone in which they are found further south.

Opposite page: *A Muttaburrasaurus stands tall beside the Grand Hotel at Hughenden, Queensland.*
Left: *The gaping jaw of the giant Kronosaurus creates a stunning entrance to a museum displaying over 100 million years of fossil history from the Richmond area in Queensland.*

FACES OF THE ARIDLANDS

The human face is the single most photographed subject on earth. Even though we are a single species, our many cultures and expressions create a never-ending smorgasbord of lens fodder. I remember my very early attempts at photographing strangers: I was nervous and the shots I took reflected my discomfort, not theirs. As time passed, I learnt to relax by simply being myself, and I let myself drift into the lives of the people I was photographing.

In the Australian outback this is easy – most people are very friendly and outgoing, although they are sometimes suspicious at first. In 1983, I was hired to spend a year photographing the characters outback. I met some fine people – gold, iron ore and opal miners, fettlers, bush mechanics, outback artists, graziers, retired cameleers, publicans, dam builders, ringers, rough riders, indigenous people, horse breakers, helicopter pilots, rodeo kings, pastoralists, road-train drivers, mission priests, boxing troupe fighters – they were tough and compassionate, rough and cultured, and all Australian. Each has a story to tell and each face reflects that story.

One thing I learned outback is never, ever judge a person on appearance. I have been privileged to meet people who, for all their eccentricities and weather-beaten exteriors, are truly outstanding individuals.

Opposite page: *A grazier.*

Top left: *A cattlewoman at the campfire.*

Bottom left to right: *A ringer; an outback mechanic; a retired cameleer.*

PLAYING OUTBACK

Outback people know hard work: with that there is little argument. When it comes to play, however, they can really let go, pulling out all stops. Horse events – gymkhanas, races, rodeos and especially those events sponsoring an organisation that benefits the community, such as the Royal Flying Doctor Service – can be very well attended even though the local population may be only a few souls. The horse race above was one such event at William Creek, on the Oodnadatta Track, between Oodnadatta and Marree. The tiny community of four swelled to more than five hundred vigorous characters from as much as 500 km away.

Above left: *Spear-throwing competition, Katherine, Northern Territory.*

Above right: *The William Creek Races, South Australia.*

Opposite page: *Fred Brophy's famous Outback Boxing Troupe at Birdsville, Queensland, for the races.*

FEED THE PEOPLE MEAT

"Eat meat!" is the slogan of much of the outback. Socially, a vegetarian gets a hard time because, if you knock back a steak, you are deemed to be a bit soft. Tolerance levels for softies might not be high, but, as a teetotaller, I have survived many social occasions – perhaps because I'm a fast talker and always seem to be busy with my camera.

The media would have us believe that the outback is a man's world. Don't believe it for a minute! The face they choose as representative may be male, but, in mining towns, fettlers camps and on cattle stations, women work as hard as the men, and often alongside them.

Opposite page: *An Aboriginal ringer on the Barkly Tableland in the Northern Territory, at the end of a three-week muster. The cattle had not seen people for more than five years.*
Left, top to bottom: *Locals get the point across in William Creek, South Australia; a tongue-in-cheek sign for the butcher shop at Halls Creek in the Kimberley, Western Australia.*

CONFRONTING SPACE

The abandoned rusting car, the lonely grave on an endless plain with nothing for company but dust, wind and flies… these are symbols of our attempts to conquer a harsh land. They are in sharp contrast to pretty wildflower carpets and romantic, light-dappled gorges. Seventy-five per cent of Australia is arid and semi-arid, and, of that vast area, only a very small part could be termed picturesque. Areas such as the gibber deserts of south-western Queensland, northern South Australia and the bottom end of the Northern Territory are little more than flat or gently undulating dirt, sand and stones. But if they are not picturesque, they have their own, austere beauty and even grandeur.

This is a landscape I love to wander and I have taken friends out there, some from other countries, and some urban Australians. Never having known such space before, some find the sensation quite disturbing. To heighten this experience, I encourage them to walk a little distance alone, just to sit and stare. It can be a great way to meet oneself, way out there in silent solitude, with the gibbers, the flies and maybe a lone eagle high in the sky.

Creative artists and musicians gain inspiration from the "emptiness" of the outback. On one occasion while I was driving over the Nullarbor Plain, I met a group of music teachers using the space to inspire a song they would later share with the kids at Cook, a tiny fettlers' town.

Above, left to right: *An abandoned car; an old miner's cottage; a lonely grave – all symbols of the harshness of Australia's vast outback.*
Right: *Musicians gather inspiration from the space of the Nullarbor near Cook, South Australia.*

CORRUGATED LIVING

A great deal of Australia's history can be associated with the story of corrugated iron. Within a few years of its invention and patent in Britain in the 1820s, corrugated iron was imported to Australia. During the gold-rushes of the 1850s, immigrants brought sheets of corrugated iron with them in packing cases, each component numbered for easy assembly. It is light and easy to assemble, and, when galvanised, corrugated iron withstands the sometimes harsh Australian weather conditions. During the First World War, manufacturing began in Australia. By the Second World War, Australia was exporting it to Britain.

Although corrugated iron is an ideal building material in some ways, it can be as hot as hell. I have interviewed people in their unlined corrugated iron shacks in kangaroo-shooting camps and mining settlements, and how they survive is beyond me. Heat of up to 55°C is not my scene – I'm a 16°C person! But there's nothing to compare with the sound of rain thundering down on a corrugated iron roof.

Above: A *miner's cottage, Ravenswood, Queensland.*
Opposite page: *Corrugated living in the hot, arid world of Cloncurry, western Queensland. Note the tropical motifs.*

Opposite page: *Masterpiece on corrugated iron, Mingenew, Western Australia.*
Above, left to right: *Children's art decorates a water tank at the Angorichina Village School, South Australia; life-sized corrugated iron camels grace the main street at Norseman, Western Australia.*

CORRUGATED ART

With so many corrugated iron buildings, not just homes but woolsheds, pubs, churches and water tanks, it is understandable that these surfaces would attract artists, whether painters or sculptors. So, wandering outback I like to keep an eye out for corrugated art, whatever form it might take.

Corrugated iron is now a well-recognised medium for creating sculpture among the Australian arts community. The corrugated iron camels are a recent addition to the main street of Norseman in south-eastern Western Australia. These innovative structures were erected to celebrate the importance of the One-humped Camel in the settlement of the Australian outback.

THE ONE-HUMPED HERO

Feral camels abound in the desert, and the culture that goes with them is still alive and well. In fact, Australia is the only place on earth where wild One-humped Camels (Dromedaries) can still be found. Researchers have estimated that, by 2015, over 1 000 000 camels will roam Australia's outback.

If you are prepared to hang about in towns like Marree, South Australia, you will meet old men who have the blood of the Afghan cameleers flowing in their veins. A little nudging, and they may have a yarn with you. As they talk, you'll imagine their trudging for days up the Birdsville track and beyond, carting vital supplies and long-awaited mail. You'll feel the bitter cold of desert nights, and you'll know the fear felt by the cameleer when jagged lightning sets off a bolt among the camels.

These weather-beaten old men were masters of the desert. By day, camels' long shadows floated over red, undulating dunes, white saltpans and glittering brown gibber plains. At night, they navigated by the stars, a convoy in a sea of sand, in silence broken only by the creaking leather of saddles and harnesses, thudding hsh-hsh-hsh of feet on the ground, and the groaning of a stubborn lead camel as it sensed a long-awaited campsite ahead.

Opposite page, far left: *Murals celebrate the pioneer role the One-humped Camel played in settling Australia – top, Alice Springs, Northern Territory, and bottom, Ravensthorpe, Western Australia.*
Opposite page, right: *A study in haughty disdain – the camel.*
Above: *In many outback areas visitors queue for a first-hand experience on the back of a One-humped Hero. This photograph was taken on the desert coast at Broome, Western Australia.*

OUTBACK – A CULTURE OF ITS OWN

Coast-dwelling urbanites are likely to pass through outback towns muttering
something like, "What on earth do people who live out here do? I'd be bored stiff."
The people of the outback would probably react the same way toward life in the cities
– but perhaps it would be phrased differently.

The social life in outback towns and among people who live on stations,
sometimes hundreds of kilometres from town, is probably just as rich as that of their
urban counterparts, but comes in short, action-packed bursts. There is a real sense of
community, even though each tiny population hub may be isolated. Heading into
town for an event or to shop is a big occasion, and so everyone makes the most of
every chance. When I pull in and sit in a café, I can't help but notice the camaraderie,
the feeling of belonging, that flows. Everyone knows everyone else – there's always a
wave, a nod and a smile. It is much harder to develop this sense of community in
cities!

In 2002, to celebrate the Year of the Outback, the outback folk did a little
exporting of their culture to the "big smoke". Ned Kelly, bushranger and cult figure,
"Priscilla, Queen of the Desert", complete with bus, and a stockman and his stock
were among the hundreds of floats and marchers that got a great reception as they
passed down city streets.

Top right, left to right: *The "Ned Kelly Gang", in memory of one of Australia's more popular
folk law icons; a suntanned ringer supports the parade's Outback theme.*
Right: *"Priscilla, Queen Of The Desert" honours a film that has now become a classic.*
Opposite page, top left and clockwise: *A curious face peers from a mural, Quorn, South
Australia; Alice Springs, the unofficial capital of the Red Centre, Northern Territory; in Broken Hill,
a major mining town (silver, lead and zinc) in western New South Wales; a welcoming sign,
Oodnadatta, South Australia; another view of Broken Hill; a roadside sign warns of camels,
wombats and kangaroos; (centre) negotiating a mob of sheep.*

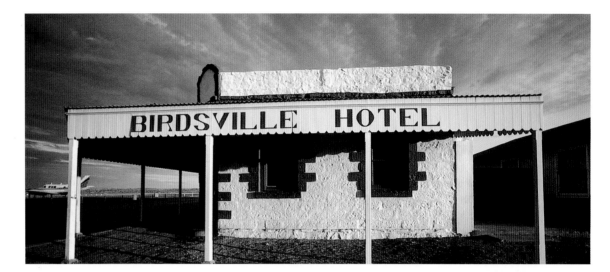

ICONIC PUBS

Australians have long recognised the importance of hotels as historic landmarks in rural and regional communities. In small country towns, where the local area may cover tens of thousands of square kilometres, many old pubs are the focus of social life, networks and debate on local issues.

For years I have been stopping to make images of classic old pubs. Some of them are heart-stoppers, glowing tall and proud in the golden light of early morning or late afternoon.

The size and grandeur of the older country pubs also serves to remind us of a bygone age, a time when wandering salesmen stayed at the local, when wool was "a pound a pound", and when the local town provided virtually all the goods and services a family needed. These days, the pubs that survive do so on the back of the tourist dollar.

Right, top to bottom: *The Birdsville Pub in south-west Queensland is possibly Australia's best-known outback pub; the Silverton Hotel, Silverton, New South Wales, site of many films and TV commercials; the oldest pub in the Northern Territory, the Daly Waters Hotel.*

Opposite page: *My choice as grandest – Imperial Hotel, Ravenswood, Queensland.*

THE ART OF STUFF

Sure, the outback has its recognised artists, but the art that attracts me is art created when people do not even know they are making the stuff – the creative expressions of ringers and mechanics, miners and truckers.

I will argue long and hard that, by my definition, they create real art. For me, art is made for the sake of the piece, without thought of applause, a picture frame or thousands of dollars. Outback art may be a sign on a fence or an old, strategically placed rubber tyre. It may be two old bikes hanging on a galvanised iron wall, a house built of bottles, or a now-useless object stacked beside another discard… Or it can be rubber-tyre swans and a collection of wind vanes in a front yard.

You can see bush art everywhere, at every station homestead, and country towns are full of it. I love the stuff and cannot resist pulling out my camera whenever another collectable comes into sight.

The lot on the opposite page is a small part of the most impressive collection I have seen. It comes from Coolgardie in Western Australia. The collector gathered so much over so many years that his house was full and he was forced to move into his caravan – the caravan itself is a collector's item.

Right, top to bottom: *Memorabilia gathers in many outback pubs as patrons make "donations"; an artfully decorated house at Jericho, central Queensland; a house of bottles, Lightning Ridge, New South Wales.*
Opposite: *A prize-winning collection from Coolgardie, Western Australia.*

BUSH KIDS

How can you overlook the children you meet as you wander the outback? Their enthusiasm is infectious, impossible to forget! I have taken town kids outback who were blown away by the seeming emptiness and lack of "stuff to do". Of course, outback youngsters get up to vastly different "stuff" from their urban cousins. My observation is that bush kids do not stand around long – after all, they have horses and bikes to ride, trucks to drive, waterholes to swim in, rivers to fish and wild gorges to explore.

Opposite page, top left and clockwise: Escaping the sun, William Creek, South Australia; kids from the Boulia school, western Queensland; a young ringer from central Queensland; playing in the wet, Northern Territory; a Coen kid; South-Australian footballer; children from Kalumburu, the Kimberley, Western Australia.

Left: Learning to ride, Jericho, Queensland.

Above: Bush kids from all over.

During recent trips I found the quantity, quality and depth of children's art that expressed their daily culture fascinating.

Art is displayed in school yards, on shop walls and on abandoned buildings of all shapes and sizes.

THE THREAT OF FERALS

In the 200 years since Europeans arrived in Australia, 17 species of mammals have become extinct and another 22 species are now in danger of disappearing. Many of these lived in Australia's vulnerable arid zones. Introduced rabbits, sheep, goats, donkeys, hares, camels and horses have damaged or destroyed many of Australia's fragile desert habitats, putting their resident mammals at risk. Cats and foxes, backed up by feral domestic dogs and Dingos, have accounted for many more victims. Researchers working in the Bulloo district of south-east Queensland estimated that the area supports 20 000 feral cats. Gut samples from a selection of these predators revealed that each could be expected to devour up to three native mammals or birds a day.

Schemes to breed threatened animals in captivity, and then release them in the wild will, I believe, only work if the release habitat is securely fenced, thoroughly cleansed of feral animals and restored to its pre-1788 state.

Above, top left and clockwise: *A Mallee Fowl working its huge nest; an endangered Mala Wallaby; Burrowing Bettong; Bilby.*
Opposite page: *The Numbat was once distributed widely across southern aridlands, but it is now restricted to a very small area in south-western Western Australia. It is highly endangered.*

A RARE LITTLE WALLABY

The gorgeous little Bridled Nailtail Wallaby was once the most common small macropod of arid Victoria, New South Wales and Queensland, but for years it was thought to be extinct. Then, in 1973, a colony was discovered in central Queensland. It was when I was working for Queensland National Parks, and I was sent out to photograph the wallabies, but found them incredibly shy and unapproachable. So it was with great joy that I finally was able to draw focus on one in 1999.

These Bridled Nailtail Wallabies were photographed at Scotia in far western New South Wales. Here, as part of the Earth Sanctuaries Wildlife Conservation Program, they are being bred to supplement the mere 300 or so animals that are estimated to survive in the wild.

While the clearing of habitat is this wallaby's primary enemy, the fox, feral dog and Dingo are important predators. Unlike the larger macropods, which hop great distances when alarmed, this little creature will usually flee only 10–30 m before hiding beneath a spinifex clump. Crouching and "freezing" in silence, it is a sitting target for any predator with a keen sense of smell.

Above: *When disturbed, the Bridled Nailtail Wallaby hops a little way and hides.*
Right: *A young Bridled Nailtail Wallaby.*

A HEAVYWEIGHT CHAMPION

Once I had a very physical clash with a large, male, Southern Hairy-nosed Wombat. I discovered the tough way that the species is enormously strong, and that, when headed at 40 km/h towards its burrow, it disregards anything in its path. I was left sprawling in the dirt, resolving to leap lightly out of the way next time I saw a wombat of any sort headed towards me.

Unlike the Common Wombat, which has a naked nose, the Southern Hairy-nosed has a furry muzzle. It lives in just two restricted areas of South Australia: in the far south-west, which, fortunately for the wombat, is of little interest to humans, and on a couple of sheep stations by the Murray River.

A group of these wombats may share a warren of burrows, whose entrances are large enough to admit a human. However, I feel no need to go down a burrow – wombats do not welcome intruders. Indeed, a wombat has been known to squash an invading dog between its tough-skinned backside and the burrow wall.

Left: *The Southern Hairy-nosed Wombat is Australia's heavyweight bush champion.*
Above: *The wombat's home is the sparsely vegetated world of the Nullarbor Plain in South Australia and Western Australia. (This photo was taken in a good year!)*

GORGES AS OLD AS TIME

To while away a long, hot day by lying half-naked on a smooth, deeply shaded, flat rock while staring into the jet-black water of a quiet billabong is as perfect a setting for relaxation as one could imagine. As I stare into the still water, a gentle breeze ruffles the red, gold and blue reflections of the cliffs into abstract patterns that mesmerise me. All around, the air is filled with the mournful cry of crows, the chattering twitters of Crimson Finches and the squabbling shrieks of corellas as they roost during the searing heat of another day. Dragonflies, wasps and native bees are the most obvious insects around the margins of such waterholes. Brilliantly coloured kingfishers sit on branches nearby, graceful swallows soar above the placid water, pigeons and parrots drink from it, and small songbirds seek the shelter of the fringing reeds and bushes. As nightfall approaches, wallabies, kangaroos and even Dingos may come quietly to drink their fill.

Once, the rivers that carved the gorges of central Australia were young, rushing streams. Today they are reduced to remnants, sometimes disappearing beneath rocky bars and sandy beds. The water that remains is all the more precious because of its arid surroundings. Massive upheavals within the earth created the mountain ranges carved by these rivers into the many steep-walled gorges. Some of them, like Ormiston Gorge and Pound, and Kings Canyon, are extremely dramatic.

Opposite page: *Kings Canyon.*

This page, top left and clockwise: *Simpsons Gap; Trephina Gorge; Ormiston Gorge; Glen Helen Gorge; Redbank Gorge; Palm Valley Gorge. All are in the Northern Territory.*

SENTINELS OF THE OUTBACK

The central aridlands of Australia are home to many species of eucalypt, whose extraordinary roots reach down to underground water, allowing them to flourish on the driest plains.

Eucalypts are life savers for a wide range of native creatures. Insects use them for food and shelter. Birds roost and nest amongst their leaves and in their hollows, and feed on their insect tenants and on the nectar and seeds they produce. Mammals too use their hollows as nests.

These tough-leaved trees are sometimes huge – as tall as 30 m. Standing all alone they can be extremely imposing in these empty landscapes. When travelling the long, dusty roads of central Australia, especially at sunset, I watch for isolated "king" and "queen" trees, camera at the ready.

Opposite page: *A giant River Red Gum graces the banks of the Fitzroy River, Northern Territory.*
Left: *A big male Red Kangaroo, Australia's largest terrestrial mammal, beneath a River Red Gum.*
Above: *A solitary giant, a Ghost Gum, MacDonnell Ranges, Northern Territory.*
Following pages: *River Red Gums frame a view of the Flinders Ranges, South Australia.*

GETTING HIGH ON EUCALYPTS

Heaven must be like being nestled in the branches of a eucalyptus tree at blossom time. There, in a profusion of colour, form and texture, drooping leaves create a backdrop for one of nature's most spectacular exhibitions. Among the branches feast insects of every size and shape. Nectar-feeding birds also come to stuff themselves on the fleeting abundance.

Ah, sweet bush… a gum tree in bloom is, without doubt, a nature photographer's paradise.

Opposite page: *Finke River Mallee.*

This page, top left and clockwise: *Red-flowering Gum; Salmon Gum; Bell-fruited Mallee; Coral Gum; Flockton's Mallee; Pear-fruited Mallee.*

THE DESERT COAST

When I first discovered the desert coast of Western Australia, I thought I had died and gone to heaven. The combination of the aqua-blue ocean water, the pure white beach sand and the deep red of the western desert sand smites the eye, especially in the golden light of dawn and dusk.

There are numerous areas I particularly like to visit, Nambung desert being possibly the most spectacular. The Pinnacles, an immediately recognised landform in Western Australian tourism imagery, are stunning. You cannot quite understand the beauty of this landscape, particularly in late afternoon when the shadows lurch across the golden yellow, wind-rippled sand, unless you have been there. Further north, looking at the Zuytdorp cliffs from the air, a sea of desert, undulating as far as the eye can see, is revealed. Then there is Shark Bay, site of the world-famous Monkey Mia, where encounters with wild dolphins enthral visitors and change their lives. Cape Peron National Park's western red sand cliffs are also a special and spectacular wild place (see pages 144 and 145). The desert coast continues further north, past wonderful places like Ningaloo Reef Marine Park, Eighty Mile Beach and Broome, where the rocks of renowned Gantheaume Point are little more than compacted desert sand, shell grit and beach sand that form spectacular graphic shapes.

Opposite page: *Nambung National Park in Western Australia, one of Australia's most beautifully bizarre landscapes.*

Left, top to bottom: *Zuytdorp Nature Reserve, where the rolling western desert dunes spill into the sea; spectacular examples of the passage of time, Box Hill Beach, Western Australia.*

Above, left to right: *Thorny Devil; Three-lined Knob-tail; Shingleback.*

Following pages, left to right: *The coastline of Peron Peninsula, jutting into Shark Bay.*

TROPICAL JOURNEYS

FROM AQUA BLUE OCEANS TO ANCIENT FLOODED GORGES

From the blue-green oceans of the Coral Sea off the north Queensland coast, and west across lush green mountains of the Great Dividing Range, through the Gulf Country, the Top End of the Northern Territory and down to the flooded gorges and canyons of Kimberley District, is a vast area that is Australia's tropical north. Photographically this area is like a huge theatre, offering an ever-changing stage show, a panorama of living things as diverse in species, as complex in varied habitat as anywhere on earth.

The fauna and flora of the tropics are breathtaking. The annual tropical monsoons, announcing themselves in black clouds crackling with incandescent lightning, create environments supporting a profusion of living things. From the Cape to the Kimberley, the cyclonic rains support multitudes of mammals, birds, reptiles, frogs and invertebrates, while the seas are full of marine life. This abundance of natural food has supported, for many tens of thousands of years, the rich cultures of indigenous people, some of which still flourish today.

I have so many memories of my journeys into this part of the world. Hunting elusive possums high in the trees of the tropical rainforests in the dead of night. Spending time on lonely islands in the Coral Sea, alone but for thousands of squawking seabirds all furiously protecting their eggs and chicks from birds that would make them a meal. Magic moments diving the steep drop-offs of outer reef in search of rare fish; Being lost for hours amongst lilies on the wetlands, marvelling at the complex dramas being enacted between the animal actors on this watery stage. Watching the brown land and receding waterways revitalised by the first torrential rains of the season. Meeting elders in Kakadu National Park and visiting the special sites where their ancestors made marks on ancient stone. These are memories that will remain with me forever.

A particular highlight was being invited to photograph at the Garma Festival in Arnhem Land, a festival designed to encourage the practice, preservation and maintenance of traditional dance *(bunggul),* song *(manikay),* art and ceremony on Yolngu lands in north-east Arnhem Land.

Previous pages: *Nourlangie Rock and Anbangbang Billabong, Kakadu National Park, Northern Territory.*
Opposite page: *The Town Common, Townsville, Queensland.*

BRISBANE – RIVER CITY

Brisbane, subtropical capital of Queensland, has a population of about 1.6 million and is Australia's third-largest city. Established in 1824 as a settlement to take the most intractable of convicts, it stands on the lower course of the Brisbane River.

Brisbane is constantly changing. In the twenty-odd years that I have called this city my home, I have witnessed many developments. Every time I look around me, the cityscape has altered.

Choosing to move from far-flung areas to older inner suburbs, many residents refurbish old "Queenslanders" – high-built timber houses with wide verandahs and corrugated iron roofs. Cafés, restaurants, trendy shops, theatres and pubs – places where people get together and relax, often outdoors – complete the inner-suburban picture. For nature-lovers, within reach is every habitat from coral reefs, sandy islands, wonderful subtropical rainforest and wildlife to rival all other Australian cities.

Down the centre of the city runs the Brisbane River, reflecting the towers of commerce, crossed and recrossed by bridges, with CityCats powering up and down the city reaches. On its banks are marvellous riverside walks, the Cultural Centre's Performing Arts complex, Museum, Art Gallery and State Library, the recreational complexes of South Bank and Riverside, and cliffs to climb at Kangaroo Point.

Brisbane is a city of tropical colour, especially in spring and summer, when crimson Poinciana blossom follows purple-blue Jacarandas and golden Silky Oaks. It is bounded by the waters and islands of Moreton Bay and the forested slopes of the D'Aguilar Range. To the north and south, the sweeping surf beaches of the Sunshine and Gold Coasts give way to hinterland valleys, forests, volcanic escarpments and rich farmlands. Brisbane and south-east Queensland are blessed indeed.

Opposite page: *A view of Brisbane, looking south-west across New Farm, Kangaroo Point, and the city centre to Mount Coot-tha.*
Left, top to bottom: *The Story Bridge; a CityCat plies the Brisbane River; Brisbane from Mount Coot-tha lookout; the popular beach in South Bank Parklands.*

THE FABULOUS GOLD COAST

The Gold Coast story began in 1925 when James Cavill built a hotel, the Surfers Paradise, in the sleepy seaside district of Elston. In 1933, Elston was officially renamed Surfers Paradise. Today, the Gold Coast is one of the world's great playgrounds.

Its delights include some of Australia's best wildlife parks, where jewel-bright lorikeets fly in to dine and koalas can be seen in the treetops. World-Heritage-listed stands of magnificent subtropical rainforest are home to ancient trees, unique birds and animals and scenic waterfalls.

The long, sweeping beaches are the tideline-walking mecca of Australia. Thousands of city-stressed holiday escapees from abroad and from all points in Australia, ease their tensions with a stroll along the tideline.

Poets, writers, photographers, artists and musicians devour this seaside soul-food, but the Gold Coast is there for all to regenerate the spirit and inspire creativity.

Above: *Tide-lining – a favourite pastime on the Gold Coast.*

Right: *The Gold Coast looking south-west towards the border ranges.*

JUST WALKING IN THE RAIN

Many of my most memorable rainforest walks have been during or just after rain. At Lamington National Park in south-east Queensland, there is an extensive track system deep into the spectacular subtropical rainforest. On one of my walks, the first heavy rains fell after a long dry spell and I swear I could hear the trees and ferns joyfully welcoming the bounteous rain. The valleys were filled with mist and, before long, what had been gently flowing creeks became swift streams rushing towards some of the loveliest fern-fringed falls in Australia.

Left to right: *Gentle rain falls in a tropical rainforest; a tree frog explores for insects.*
Opposite page: *Chalahn Falls shrouded in mist, Lamington National Park and World Heritage Area, south-east Queensland.*
Following pages: *Nandroya Falls in the Palmerston Section of Wooroonooran National Park and World Heritage Area, Tropical North Queensland.*

Left to right: *A carnivorous Pitcher Plant from Cape York Peninsula; the Cooktown Orchid, flora emblem of Queensland.*

Opposite page: *The Red-eyed Tree Frog.*

FRUSTRATION, AGONY AND ECSTASY

Fish must surely be the most difficult species to photograph. Or so I used to think, until I began to photograph birds, especially those living in dark places such as rainforests. To call it frustrating is an understatement – there is considerable difficulty photographing shy, fast-moving, often well-camouflaged birds in a dark forest where it is not easy to move around. It is agony when I get to within photographing distance and, while I'm focusing, the bird decides to fly away! An even more painful experience is spending hours closing in, getting a shot, then finding I have under-exposed the picture! If everything goes my way, and I think I just might have a good picture, I worry until I can send the film for developing. Then if the film comes back from the lab and the shot is exactly as I wanted… that's ecstasy!

Left to right: *Rose-crowned Fruit-Dove; female Eclectus Parrot; Regent Bower Bird.*
Opposite page: *Rainbow Lorikeet feed on the nectar of the tropical Umbrella Tree. All images from Tropical North Queensland.*

GLIDING WITH THE BUTTERFLIES

Extreme patience is required to photograph butterflies, which, like all insects and unlike birds and mammals, give no warning of their intent. Roosting birds about to take off and kangaroos about to bolt will show tension, giving at least some warning, but butterflies give none. You can hold a butterfly in focus waiting for it to spread its wings until your arms feel like they will drop off. The second you relax, off they go!

Tropical rainforests are spectacular places to view butterflies, particularly during the spring mating season when activity is at its highest. An experience that should not be missed, and an exciting way to view these rainforest jewels, is the Skyrail cablecar ride as it passes low over the canopy of the rainforest behind Cairns.

Opposite page, left, top to bottom: *A female Common Eggfly; a Red Lacewing showing its underwings; a Red Lacewing from above; a Ulysses Butterfly on frangipani flowers.*
Centre: *A fan palm forest, Mission Beach, Queensland.*
Above, top to bottom: *A Skyrail gondola glides above the forest canopy; a Cairns Birdwing.*

THE GREAT BARRIER REEF

The Great Barrier Reef Marine Park and World Heritage Area stretches 2000 km along the Queensland coast from Lady Elliot Island to Torres Strait. Within its tropical waters lies the world's largest system of coral reefs and the world's largest structure built by living organisms. On its eastern rim, long ribbons and platforms of coral rise 200 m above the continental shelf, creating a barrier to the forces of the Pacific Ocean. Behind this great outer wall is an inner labyrinth of reefs, lagoons, sand cays and deep channels. Further inshore, coral reefs fringe the coastline and high continental islands.

The foundations of this vast empire are the millions of hard limestone skeletons secreted by generations of tiny animals known as coral polyps. A thin layer of these colourful animals forms the living, growing part of a reef. While the bulk of a coral reef is not alive, there is an abundance of life in and around it. An underwater version of Alice's Wonderland, the sheer numbers, colours and shapes of marine plants and animals defy the imagination.

About 1500 species of fish have been found, ranging from delicate anemonefish to the giant Manta Ray. The warm reef waters are also the winter breeding ground of Humpback Whales. In late spring the coral cays attract thousands of nesting seabirds and turtles, and migratory wading birds arrive from as far away as Siberia seeking food and rest.

With more than 2900 coral reefs and some 900 islands and cays, this World Heritage Area offers a variety of Great Barrier Reef experiences. You do not need scuba diving skills – a simple facemask and snorkel will do, and a marine biology degree is not a prerequisite for appreciating the reef and its inhabitants.

Right: *The Great Barrier Reef offers an endless variety of subjects to photograph.*
Opposite page: *The sparkling world of the Great Barrier Reef.*

LAGOONS

Snorkelling in coral island lagoons is a pastime open to anyone; it is wonderfully exhilarating and relaxing. The best time to snorkel is just before the turn of a high tide when the water is at its clearest. Towards the crest of a reef on the more protected side of an island may be the best spot, unless it is one of those rare windless days. I like to snorkel in the late afternoon when reef activity is at its highest. At the northern end of the Great Barrier Reef, particularly on less-visited islands, the activity can be very spectacular. During the egg-laying season, you may encounter large numbers of female turtles preparing for their night-time expedition to lay eggs. It is also a time when reef fish are particularly active.

Above: Snorkelling in coral lagoons is a stimulating way to while away the hours.

Opposite page: Lady Musgrave Island's lagoon is renowned for diving.

TAKING A TURN

Sea birds live in an extremely hazardous, highly competitive environment and have evolved to become the world's best aerial performers and successful fisherfolk. To many people, one seabird is similar to another – white with a bit of black and, if anything like Silver Gulls, they make a confounded racket! However, like most of nature's creatures, if you look closely into their lives you will find astounding behaviours and fascinating daily routines.

Two of my favourite groups are the terns and the tropicbirds: the former is a large, commonly seen family that nests primarily in tropical waters; the latter has only two family members, the White-tailed and the Red-tailed. In my early days as a wildlife photographer, I used to practise my focus and panning skills on such great subjects. On first sight, there are so many birds that you think it will be a breeze to photograph them. Within minutes, you find your 500 mm lens is not so easily manoeuvred, or focused, on such masters of the air. With patience and lots of film, the effort is worthwhile as there is little more pleasing than to peer through the magnifying glass at your newly returned images to find one, just one, of the dozens of shots, is perfect.

Above: *Black-naped Terns (left and right); Roseate Tern (centre).*

Right: *Red-tailed Tropicbird.*

Opposite page: *Crested Terns.*

MAKING DISCOVERIES

When I began to dive the deep waters of southern New South Wales in the late sixties, my enthusiasm for underwater creatures exploded. I soon discovered that many of the invertebrates and fish I captured on film had not been photographed alive, although many were preserved in museum specimen jars as the result of dredging operations. I photographed these creatures alive, in natural colour, going about their daily chores, and added some species new to science as well. My first published book, *Oceans of Life*, in 1971, was a tribute to these encounters.

Even today there is little known about most sea creatures and all knowledge gained is valuable – the underwater photographer is still a pioneer, explorer and discoverer.

Opposite page: *Divers wait to see how an anemonefish family reacts to other passing fish.*
Left, top to bottom: *The Pink Anemonefish lives in the swaying tentacles of the sea anemone, immune to the venom that is deadly to most other marine animals; a keen eye is needed to spot this tiny Porcelain Crab.*
Above: *I was overwhelmed with excitement when I found this tiny Longnose Hawkfish.*

Above, left to right: *Hard corals; Gorgonian Coral; feather stars feeding on plankton on a coral outcrop.*

Opposite page, left to right: *Vermilion spikules contrast with a soft coral's white fleshy body; the bulbous tips of a sea anemone and sunshine coral polyps in extreme close-up — these animals, like thousands forming Queensland's magnificent Great Barrier Reef, create a lifetime challenge for photographers.*

RHAPSODY IN BLUE

Some of the most exhilarating moments in my life have taken place in the vast blue space between sea-surface and sea-floor. I have experienced ecstasy simply hanging in the water, staring up at the sun blazing in luminous abstractions through the surface.

While suspended in space like this, it is awe-inspiring to be joined by sharks, Manta Rays, or whales. Meetings with these magnificent marine creatures are at the pinnacle of all my wild encounters to date. In the open ocean, they are usually wary of human encounters, however there have been times when, for brief moments, I have been allowed to join them. These sea-dwellers may pause, circle and stare, trying to identify this strange creature appearing in their saltwater kingdom. Often whales and dolphins will swim together, and during a shallow-water encounter with a very large Humpback Whale I was thrilled to see six young dolphins playfully barrel-rolling around the giant. I also experienced one Humpback swim eye to eye with me across a mere half-metre of seawater. We stared at each other, and I would love to think the whale was as fascinated by the encounter as I. Did it spend that night drifting in half-sleep as I did, deep in wonder at this remarkable experience?

Opposite page, left to right: *A giant Manta Ray glides past; a school of Bat Fish mill as one entity; two Bottlenose Dolphins briefly visit.*
Left: *A diver "flies the blue".*

RAINFOREST MEETS REEF

Tropical Queensland, where two World Heritage Areas meet, is the only place in Australia where rainforest actually grows right down to the ocean's edge. It occurs in several localities, and three of my favourites are Dunk Island, Cape Tribulation and Hinchinbrook Island, each of which is a national park. It's hard to imagine more spectacular environments literally at each other's doorsteps. At dawn and dusk you wander the beach listening to a chorus of rainforest birds setting up their territories for the day, and in the afternoon snorkel clear, shallow, coral reef waters.

Opposite page, left, top to bottom: *Green Tree-frog; Lumholtz's Tree-kangaroo; Green Python.*
Centre: *Muggy Muggy Beach, Dunk Island, Queensland, where rainforest meets reef.*
Left, top to bottom: *Masked Bannerfish; Humpback Whale; soft coral.*

BEACHES FOR DREAMING

Australia has many spectacular beaches, and the tropical coasts and islands are especially endowed. Bright, hot days on long sweeps of gleaming sand washed by clear blue tropical waters are followed by warm, softly lit evenings and cool, velvet nights. This is the stuff of dreams.

Above, left to right: *Low Island off Port Douglas; Whitehaven Beach, Whitsunday Island.*

Opposite page, top to bottom: *Zoe Bay, Hinchinbrook Island; Green Island; Cape Tribulation.*

WALKING INTO PARADISE

The best, the very best, way to experience tropical paradise – or anywhere for that matter – is on foot. You can set your own pace, you can get side-tracked if you want to follow something unexpectedly interesting, you can carry as much or as little as you need, but …

… even experienced bushwalkers can find themselves in difficulties. Paradise can have its dark side. It is essential that you prepare, plan, and follow the rules. Parks and wildlife authorities will help all they can, but they do have rules that have been made for your safety and protection. That said, walking – just being – in a tropical rainforest, knowing that it harbours the greatest diversity of natural life in the country, can be a profoundly enriching experience.

Some of the most exciting, most touching, funniest, scariest and best times in my life as photographer and publisher have happened when I was on foot. Being on foot can actually mean being flat down on my stomach to focus on a delicate ground orchid, being up to my armpits in a swamp, in company with snakes and crocodiles, in order to convey the steamy, lush greenness, or, draped with camera and lenses, clambering up a steep rockface while the rock-wallabies, sure-footed and disdainful, bound on ahead.

Right: A family sets out on a five-day walk of a lifetime on Hinchinbrook Island, Queensland.

SUNRISE

In the tropical north I try not to sleep in – that would be sacrilege. Far better to enjoy the sunrise and go back to bed later if you must. While sunset is a time of magic as the cloak of night descends, a tropical sunrise, ushering in a new day, is very special. The air is cooler following the night, and I feel full of energy. If the air is thick with vapour or dust particles and the clouds have formed nicely, there might also be a sky of truly spectacular colour to shoot.

Above: *An Eastern Grey Kangaroo visits the beach at sunrise.*
Right, top to bottom: *Pandanus Palms; Coconut Palms. Both in Townsville.*
Opposite page: *Against the kaleidoscopic dawn sky, the silhouetted shape of a rock formation at Cape Hillsborough gives foreground drama to this shot.*

EXPECT THE UNEXPECTED

Lawn Hill, set in the semi-arid and remote north-western highlands of
Queensland, is an area of surprising contrasts. Beneath the vast plateau of sun-baked
limestone, freshwater springs feed the park's gorge-carving creeks. Figs and palms
crowd around deep waterholes below the gorge cut through the sandstone ridges.

There are good facilities and a 20 km walking track system at Lawn Hill Gorge.
Graded trails lead to scenic lookouts, Aboriginal cultural sites and unusual geological
formations. Off-track walking on the plateau is not difficult, but can be
uncomfortably hot during the middle of the day.

The canoe trip down the cool green waters of the gorge is relaxing and stimulating
at the same time: being totally away from the stresses of everyday life, yet being part
of such ancient landscape. At the end of the gorge, Lawn Hill and Widdalion Creeks
have, over the centuries, eroded a 50 m sandstone column, Island Stack. It forms a
perfect vantage point from which to marvel at the stark contrast of the tropical
vegetation of the national park and the surrounding undernourished country.

Dawn, dusk and night spotlighting walks are the best times to look for the
abundant bird and animal life of the park. Sunrise reveals some of Lawn Hill's living
fossils: the tranquil gorge waters are home to Freshwater Crocodiles and Northern
Snapping Turtles.

Right: *Paddling a canoe on the tranquil waters between the orange cliffs of Lawn Hill Gorge.*

BIRDS IN THEIR ELEMENT

Waterbirds have evolved a variety of body shapes, which guarantees each bird the highest level of feeding success. A species is perfectly adapted to its lifestyle, filling a habitat niche enabling a group to live together with other species in minimal competition for resources.

Late or early in the day is the best time to photograph waterbirds. At these times they are most active, bathed in soft, warm light giving depth, dimension and colour to the images. Using a telephoto lens, I like to drift quietly in a boat, sit or walk unobtrusively by the water. I may either fill the frame with a bird, or pull back to create space around my subject and include some landscape.

Photographing around water also adds another element to a composition. It is the ultimate triumph for me when the bird is in a good position, in scenic, uncluttered surroundings, and a little extra bonus when its image is mirrored in still water.

Above: *Australian Pelicans float in the dawn light with a thousand whistling-ducks.*
Right: *Egrets and Magpie Geese congregate, sometimes in tens of thousands, right across the wetlands of tropical Australia.*

Above: A preening female Jabiru (Black-necked Stork) can be recognised by its distinctive yellow eye – the male has brown eyes.

Left and right: *A Darter gives out its harsh territorial call; a juvenile Cattle Egret mantling.*
Centre, clockwise from top: *Preening keeps feathers in good order and condition for a Brolga, a Yellow-billed Spoonbill and an Australian Pelican.*

SKY FLYING

From early January to late March, monsoonal rains pour on to Arnhem Land in the Northern Territory, then spill over the escarpment on to vast floodplains and into the sea. In this Wet, the brown, heat-ravaged landscapes created by the pre-Wet build-up are transformed. Charred grasses sprout bright green then grow 2 m tall. The black, cracked mud of the plains vanishes under brown water, swaying grasses and pink lotus lilies. Towering black clouds and rolling peals of thunder herald displays of lightning to outshine any millennium fireworks.

One of the great experiences of my life was skimming across the Top End floodplains in a boat, past shadowy paperbark and pandanus and through rosy lotus flowers. I stood at the bow; arms spread wide, wind in my hair, looking at the shimmering reflections of clouds shattered into vivid abstractions by the boats passing on the endless mirror floodplain. I felt like a giant bird soaring in the sky, high on the most magnificent drug of all – adrenaline manufactured by my reaction to the natural world.

Right: *A Finch among the riverbank sedges.*

Opposite page: *The mirrored waterworld of Kakadu National Park, Northern Territory.*

LOST AMONG LILIES

At Nourlangie, in the heart of Kakadu National Park, there are several deep billabongs that hold water even at the peak of the Dry. When the country all around is parched, the Nourlangie billabongs are covered with birds. In 1978, I camped beside one of these oases. What a time I had, exploring the lost world of giant paperbark trees, wading the shallows among the pandanus, sitting watching birds and insects plundering the rich store of nectar in the flowers of drooping freshwater mangroves. It was Eden reincarnate: waterlily fields in the shallower backwaters were alive with fish, frogs, birds, butterflies, spiders, dragonflies and, yes, leeches, water pythons and file snakes. Who cared? I waded for hours, waist-deep, comforted by the fact that our Aboriginal friends were on the lookout for crocodiles, and I knew that they would spot the telltale bumps of nostrils and eyes long before I did. For six weeks I was lost among the lilies, living in a tropical wonderland where every dawn brought new and delightful experiences.

Opposite page: *Photographing a waterlily and paperbark forest in Kakadu National Park.*
Left: *The magnificent lotus lily of Australia's tropical wetlands.*
Above: *A large Saltwater Crocodile giving me the eye.*

A CLOAK OF DARKNESS

Many people visiting the tropics are disappointed when they do not see much wildlife. Certainly they see lots of birds, and perhaps a crocodile or two, but what about the smaller mammals, reptiles and frogs?

Consider that, during the day, tropical skies are full of birds of prey whose keen eyes can detect a scurrying lizard from half a kilometre away. Waiting closer to the ground are kookaburras, crows, butcherbirds and other predators. Also, sunlit hours are often very hot, especially for creatures in fur coats or with soft delicate skin such as frogs have. Under cloak of darkness, these small creatures make their move. Still constantly on the lookout for foe such as owl, frogmouth, quoll and phascogale (not to mention the feral cat and fox), they seem to stand a better chance after dark.

If you are lucky you may have a nocturnal visitor come and clean your plates off after dinner. I was camped beside an escarpment that was home to a quoll family, and one night I heard a rustle outside my tent. Peering out I could see a furry bottom and fluffy tail emerging from a very large box of breakfast cereal. Unable to open the inside packet, the quoll simply knocked the box off the table, grabbed the entire packet and headed off up the escarpment full belt! In the moonlight, all I could see was a ghostly white packet bouncing over the rocks. I drove off the following morning chuckling at the thought of the family of quolls all tucked into bed for the day, their little bellies bloated with my breakfast!

Right, top to bottom: *An elusive Giant Cave Gecko of Western Arnhem Land and the Kimberley; a nervous Long-nosed Bandicoot visits my camp to clean up my remaining Pad Thai supper; a male Red-eyed Tree-frog calls for a mate.*
Opposite page: *The Sugar Glider is a gliding possum that feeds on insects, tree sap and nectar.*

SOME DAYS ARE DIAMONDS

In 1978, I spent six weeks wandering the back tracks of Kakadu in a battered old Landcruiser. It was before the park had been declared, the roads were unsealed, and camping grounds and tourists had not yet invaded. I had a single cassette tape by John Denver, and one song seemed to capture the mood of the moment:

"Some days are diamonds, some days are stone."

That is the way of the bush. Some days are forever memorable; others simply do not work out as planned.

The Stone Country of the Top End, with its ancient ranges, escarpments and outcrops, never disappoints me. Unique to the escarpment and its outliers are creatures such as the Black Wallaroo, the Chestnut-quilled Rock Pigeon, the Rock Ringtail Possum and the mighty Oenpelli Python.

Aboriginal people used the Stone Country for a multitude of purposes. The caves provided cover in the Wet, the ledges served as sacred burial sites, and the smooth walls formed panels on which to record events and sacred art.

The Stone Country is diamond-bright in its ancient magnificence.

Opposite page: *There is perhaps no better place to get an impression of the sheer drama of the Arnhem Land Plateau than at Nitmiluk National Park in the Northern Territory.*
Left: *A wallaroo pauses while feeding in the late afternoon light, a last-moment encounter that concluded a "diamond day".*
Following pages: *Another adventure begins in Katherine Gorge, Northern Territory.*

Above, both pages, left to right: *Waterfalls of the Top End of the Northern Territory. Wangi Falls and Florence Falls, Litchfield National Park;*

Twin Falls, Kakadu National Park.

IN SEARCH OF A CULTURE

In many Aboriginal communities, there are people who have a passionate desire to keep their culture alive. Their language, art and stories, their food – every aspect of life – are special to them, and have been for thousands of years. Indigenous cultures are stronger in some parts of Australia than others, but they are important to indigenous people everywhere. I find much to admire, and sometimes to envy, in such well-defined cultural richness.

The very special features that have made a deep and lasting impression on me over the years include the care and attention that Aboriginal people give their children. There is lots of touching, support, and patience. I am also deeply moved by the level of forgiveness Aboriginal people are prepared to offer towards those who have done them wrong. Saying "sorry" is an important practice in Aboriginal cultures. I wish this type of healing had a similar emphasis in our culture.

To me, most important is indigenous peoples' regard for their land and all the plants and animals that live on and in it. This respect is deep and very spiritual.

Right and opposite page: *Across the tropical north, Aboriginal art can be found in caves and shelters. It should be respected by anyone who chances upon it: it is not there for the entertainment of travellers, but is an integral part of a culture.*

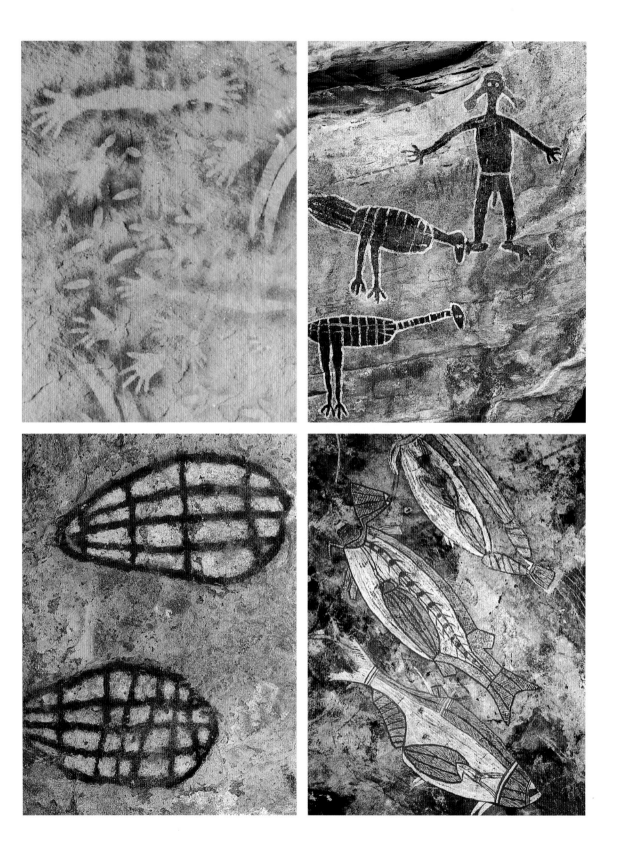

KEEPING CULTURE ALIVE

Yolngu culture in north-east Arnhem Land is among the oldest living cultures on earth, stretching back more than 40 000 years.

Regarded as one of Australia's most significant indigenous festivals, the Garma Festival of Traditional Culture will attract about 20 clan groups from north-east Arnhem Land, as well as representatives from clan groups and neighbouring indigenous peoples throughout Arnhem Land and the Northern Territory.

The Garma Festival is a celebration of the Yolngu cultural inheritance. The Garma ceremony is aimed at sharing knowledge and culture, opening people's hearts to the message of the land at Gulkula. The site at Gulkula has profound meaning for Yolngu. Set in a stringy-bark forest with views to the Gulf of Carpentaria, Gulkula is where the ancestor Ganbulabula brought the *yidaki* (didjeridu) into being among the Gumatj people. The festival is designed to encourage the practice, preservation and maintenance of traditional dance *(bunggul)*, song *(manikay)*, art and ceremony on Yolngu lands in north-east Arnhem Land.

The festival is an important step in the establishment of the Garma Cultural Studies Institute, to be built on the site at Gulkula.

Opposite page, left and above: *Yolngu culture being celebrated through dance and crafts at the Garma Festival.*

DARWIN'S WAY

Capital of the Northern Territory, Darwin has a population of around 90 000 and is Australia's fourteenth-largest city. Founded in 1869 as the centre for a northern cattle industry, it occupies a peninsula jutting into Beagle Gulf, with Frances Bay on the east and Fannie Bay on the west. Space has never been a problem in Darwin, and the suburbs sprawl around a vast civil and military airport. The climate is tropical. The Dry, which extends through the middle of the year, is pleasantly warm and lacking in rain. The Build-up, which leads to the wet season, is hot and oppressive, and the Wet, which breaks in November or December and lasts until March, brings torrential rains.

Life in Darwin centres on outdoor activities, and the city's gardens are outstanding and its parks well used. Dining on the Wharf Precinct, strolling along the Esplanade during a rosy sunset or joining festivities such as Mindil Markets are splendid pleasures of Darwin life. The population of Darwin is multicultural and exciting, local festivals include colourful ethnic dress, music and dance styles, and sensational cooking flavours originating all around the world.

It is only recently that I began to stay in Darwin, rather than use it merely as a launching pad to surrounding wilderness areas. I have found Darwin people extremely hospitable. Owning a hectare or three of bushland, then setting up a cool concrete bungalow surrounded by wide shady verandas, is the objective of many. Soon there's a vegetable garden; before long, a mini jungle. A few birdbaths attract nocturnal mammals, and, during the day, birds sing and splash beneath the shade of fast-growing tropical trees. Weekends are for fishing, exploring the wilds, or simply relaxing on the veranda with friends, a yarn and a good old Aussie barbecue to enjoy.

Opposite page: *Images from the Darwin Festival, a celebration of a multicultural population, surround an aerial of Darwin, the capital of the Northern Territory.*
Left: *Children play in a fiery sea beneath the setting sun, Fannie Bay, Darwin.*

LUSTING FOR NEW LANDSCAPE

Excitement mounted when I found a helicopter and, more importantly, a pilot to take me into a remote area I had spotted three years earlier while flying at high altitude.

The area lies south of the massive Arnhem Land Plateau on the Gulf of Carpentaria, and here, over thousands of years, torrential monsoons have cascaded over sandstone, leaving giant pillars as tall as high-rise buildings. These pillars of stone can look like a "lost city", and the drama of their presence is heightened by the fact that the surrounding landscape is virtually flat, often quite sparsely vegetated woodland so typical of the Northern Territory's Top End.

Some of the "lost cities" are vast; others, like the one featured here, are no larger than a city block. This "city" had its own spring and monsoonal rainforest and even during the heat of late morning the birds were enthusiastically singing. They were probably announcing they had been invaded by some giant alien space ship.

Left: These towering sandstone residuals have been created over the aeons by wind and water. This comparatively small area near Nathan River, Northern Territory, has its own spring and monsoon rainforest.

INSPIRED BY NATURE

Covering an area of over 200 000 ha, Purnululu National Park has a geological history of 360 million years. The area is comparatively new in terms of European visitation and, before 1983, was known only to stockmen and local Aboriginal communities. Aboriginal people, inspired to create paintings on the landscape itself, occupied this area for many thousands of years; today their artworks remain. The traditional owners of Purnululu, known also as the Bungle Bungles, are still inspired to paint, although these days their art is more likely to be found on anything from petrol pumps to wheelie bins.

Although it appears solid, the sandstone of the striped domes of the Bungle Bungles is extremely fragile. A "skin" on the sandstones holds the sand grains in place, but if this is damaged or removed, the sandstones erode. The darker bands are coloured by algal growth on the more permeable layers that allow water to seep into the stone.

The best time to visit is during the dry cooler mid-year months when the bushland surrounding the outcrops comes alive and the shrubs burst into flower. If you ever do take this exciting journey, the effect this wonderful wild place will have on you will amaze you. You may well find yourself creating some sort of memorabilia, perhaps a photo, artwork, or even a poem, to take away with you. Purnululu is a jewel in the Australian landscape crown.

Right, top: *The stark, dramatic shapes of Boab trees is highlighted by the setting sun.*
Right, bottom, left to right: *Children's art on a wheelie bin; an inspired petrol bowser.*
Both shots from Halls Creek.
Opposite page: *Purnululu from the air.*

Above: *The Lennard River runs through the gorge in Windjana Gorge National Park, the Kimberley, Western Australia.*

Above: *The river cascades over the escarpment in Mitchell River National Park, the Kimberley, Western Australia.*
Following pages: *Repeating patterns from Geikie Gorge National Park, Western Australia.*

A PERSONAL JOURNEY

I was born in Great Britain in 1945 to Australian parents and when I was one year old we moved to Melbourne. By the time I was five, we had settled in Adelaide. My school years were unhappy, so I left early to work as a jackeroo, and, not long after, I took up an apprenticeship to a gunsmith, a short-lived job from which I was dismissed for fighting.

In 1962, my life took a sudden turn, as a result of a chance encounter with Igo Oak, a pioneer Australian underwater photographer. The meeting with Igo took place on an expedition with the South Australian Museum to Kangaroo Island. I was sixteen, and had been invited on the trip to assist the museum in the collection of marine fish: at the time I was a keen and quite accomplished spear fisherman. It was during this trip that Igo set about turning my interest from killing fish to photographing them. And so began my life-long love affair with photographing fish, a pastime that fully occupied the first fifteen years of my photographic activities. I lived in Adelaide until I moved back east to join the Royal Australian Navy at the age of eighteen.

During my early years in the Navy, training to be a search and rescue diver, I was drafted to Jervis Bay which, to a keen underwater photographer, was like being sent straight to heaven! I started to share my exploits with others through magazine articles and symposium presentations. As a result of the public exposure of these early images, my self-confidence increased, particularly when I learnt that many of the marine animals I was photographing were new to science.

I was thirty years of age before I took a picture on land. For the first time, I had a job that gave my life meaning. The task was to photograph the wildlife of Queensland for the National Parks and Wildlife Service. This exciting opportunity gave me the chance to enhance my skills and learn techniques for photographing a wide range of animals in all of the State's varied ecosystems, from the Great Barrier Reef to the western deserts.

After five years photographing Queensland I was keen to explore every possible aspect of the Australian landmass, its people and their varied activities as they related to the landscape. In 1984, my publisher closed its doors and in 1985 I formed my own company. Since then my dream has been to share Australia with the world.

While many of my publications are pictorial books, my primary motivation has been to reach Australian children through books and other materials based on Australian natural history. In a way, I have come full circle – it was the images in National Geographic magazine that ignited my interest in nature when I was a small child.

Opposite page, clockwise from top left: *A spear-fisherman, 1960; photographing Kakadu, 1978; with my first underwater camera that took in-focus pictures, 1965; underwater filming for the ABC, 1975; while working for Queensland National Parks, 1976; photographing fish in Jervis Bay, 1971; photographing wildflowers, 2000.*
Left: *Photographing in the Kimberley, 1987.*

BEHIND THE PHOTOGRAPHS

I was first attracted to photography because I had a desire to communicate exactly what I saw. Composition was irrelevant, as long as the subject was within the frame of the picture. I was completely engrossed in collecting numbers of fish species, so the photographs were all of fish side-on to the camera lens, as close and as detailed as possible. Later, my interest in fish broadened to all marine animals, and for fifteen years the underwater world consumed me.

My first camera was a plastic Mako Shark, a small, round 120 mm job, branded "tested to thirty metres". It leaked constantly at one metre! In 1963, I bought the first Nikonos camera released by Nikon. In 1965, I progressed to a twin lens reflex camera in a perspex housing and made my first serious, in-focus, colour photographs. I wanted large format and a sharp lens to record crisp detail, so I used a Rollie-marine twin lens reflex, then a Hasselblad in a custom metal housing. This equipment stayed with me until I changed back to 35 mm with the Nikon RS Underwater camera system.

In 1975, when I began top-side photography, I started with a Minolta, and soon changed to Nikon, a brand I have been faithful to ever since. Today I use a Nikon 5 with a variety of lenses for wildlife photography. For landscape photography, I use the 6 x 7 format Mamiya RZ and the Mamiya 7.

I like large format, especially for landscapes, because of the extra detail obtainable when the image is cropped. Depending on the opportunity in front of me, I may work with both 6 x 7 and 35 mm formats at once.

Other than underwater and at night, I have only recently begun to use electronic flash. With the new technology, fill-flash allows more opportunities to shoot in difficult lighting conditions. I constantly use a tripod and cable release, and, while I used to use 64 ISO Kodachrome, I now use mostly 100 ISO Kodak transparency film.

When I'm taking a photograph, I think how an image will be used, approaching my work as a storyteller, and I try not to overlook any obvious opportunity. I make the majority of my photographic decisions on the spur of the moment.

Right: *Photographing the Antarctic Beech forest in Lamington National Park.*

Opposite page: *Our unique and beautiful wildflowers are a particular interest of mine.*

ACKNOWLEDGING THE JOURNEY

First and foremost, I have my late mother to thank for having implanted in me at a very young age a passionate desire to communicate visually. I also thank my father for having the insight to buy me an underwater facemask for Christmas when I was nine. That gift transported me to another world. The first camera I ever used was handed to me by Igo Oak in 1962, and it was his considerable encouragement that lit a flame of desire in me to make photography my life's work. The Royal Australian Navy's tough Diving Chiefs Bill Fitzgerald and Joe Flarity taught me discipline and how to focus energy in the very hardest physical way possible. These skills remain with me and have influenced me throughout my life.

My very early underwater photography, natural history and publishing careers were encouraged enormously by Reg Lipson and Barry Andrewartha. My keen interest in the natural history of marine fishes was encouraged by Fisheries scientist, Dr David Pollard, and renowned underwater naturalist, Neville Coleman.

In 1975, Peter Davie had the idea that I should photograph for the Queensland National Parks and Wildlife Service. He introduced me to Peter Ogilvie and, as a result of Peter's encouragement, my world changed dramatically. I began to take pictures on land! My development as a photographer and interpreter of terrestrial wildlife was supported by National Parks staff, Damian McGreevy, Peter Stanton, Dr Greg Gorden and Dr John Winton.

Des Power of Channel Nine and Rod Davis of Rigby Publishing introduced me to the tough world of commercial publishing and encouraged my commercial career. The birth of my own publishing company was supported by Jan Parish, who worked beside me tirelessly for twelve years, building Steve Parish Publishing into the company that it is today. I would also acknowledge the camaraderie afforded by my nature and photography mates Allan Fox, Ian Morris, Stan Breeden and Peter Slater.

This book was produced entirely in my publishing studio in Brisbane and I thank all my staff, and in particular the Publishing Team: Richard Watkins, Ann Wright, Pat Slater, Leanne Staff, Kate Lovett, Phil Jackson; also Philip Hayson in providing past field photographic assistance. A special thanks to Catherine Prentice, a partner on many exploits in this book who also provided challenging editorial comment. Grateful thanks are due to the Yothu Yindi Foundation who invited me to the Garma Festival and gave me permission to include some of the images I took there in this book.

I must also thank those many Australians who gave me a shove in the right direction, shared a cuppa, pointed out an orchid or where an elusive bird was nesting – thank you all for being part of my journey.

Opposite: *An Egret flies by a jabiru in Kakadu, Northern Territory. This is my favourite "journey" picture.*
Top: *I was collecting fish and Igo Oak was photographing them. He handed me his camera during the dive, and it was then that I took my very first picture. I was sixteen.*
Bottom: *Eight years later I returned to Adelaide to show Igo my new camera.*

TORRES STRAIT

TIMOR SEA

DARWIN

Melville Is
Bathurst Is

Arnhem
Land

Groote Eylandt

GULF OF
CARPENTARIA

Cape
York
Pen

Great Barrier Reef

CORAL SEA

Cooktown

Cape Tribulation

Cairns

Top End

Daly R

Katherine

Roper R

Mornington Is

Riversleigh

Alligator Rivers

Barkly Tableland

Wyndham

Ord R

Kimberley
Division

Derby

Fitzroy R

Halls
Creek

Broome

NORTHERN
TERRITORY

Victoria R

Georgina R

QUEENSLAND

Mount Isa

Mt Mistake

Townsville

INDIAN OCEAN

Great Sandy Desert

Port Hedland

Tanami Desert

Boulia

Great Dividing Range

Burdekin R

Montebello Is

Exmouth
Gulf

Ningaloo Reef

Hamersley Range

Gibson Desert

MacDonnell Ranges

Alice Springs

Diamantina R

Tropic of Capricorn

Rockhampton

SHARK BAY

Ashburton R

WESTERN AUSTRALIA

Warburton Range

Birdsville

Cooper Creek

Charleville

Condamine R

Burnett R

Gascoyne R

Carnarvon

Simpson
Desert

Fraser Is

Bernier Is
Dorre Is
Dirk Hartog Is

Monkey Mia

Murchison R

Musgrave Ranges

Innamincka

Bulloo R

BRISBANE

Moreton Bay

Lake Eyre

SOUTH
AUSTRALIA

Great Victoria Desert

Flinders Ranges

Darling R

Macquarie R

Clarence R

Coff's Harbour

PACIFIC
OCEAN

Houtman
Abrolhos

Geraldton

Nullarbor Plain

Broken Hill

NEW SOUTH WALES

Hunter R

Lord Howe Is

INDIAN
OCEAN

Kalgoorlie

Eucla

EYRE
PEN

GREAT AUSTRALIAN BIGHT

Lachlan R

Newcastle

PERTH

Rottnest Is

Darling Range

Swan R

Spencer Gulf

ADELAIDE

Murrumbidgee R

CANBERRA

Great Dividing Range

SYDNEY

Cape Naturaliste

Blackwood R

Esperance

Recherche Archipelago

Big Desert

Murray R

ACT

Cape Leeuwin

SOUTHERN OCEAN

Kangaroo Is

VICTORIA

TASMAN
SEA

MELBOURNE

PORT PHILLIP
BAY

Wilson's Promontory

Cat Is
Flinders Island

BASS STRAIT

King Island

Queenstown

Launceston

TASMANIA

HOBART

Limits of Continental Shelf

The hamlet, No Where Else, is in northern Tasmania. I saw a sign in a magazine for Somewhere Else on Eyre Peninsula, South Australia, and drove hundreds of kilometres out of my way to photograph it. Alas, someone had pinched it!

Text, photography and photographic design: Steve Parish
Photographs of Steve: Basia Meder, Les Parish, Louise Parish, Connie Parish, Les Gilbert, John Dawe, Jan Parish and Jill Oak
Text: Steve Parish, with Catherine Prentice and Pat Slater, SPP
Design and finished art: Leanne Staff, SPP
Print production: Phil Jackson, SPP
Marketing: Ann Wright, SPP
Editorial management: Kate Lovett, SPP
Editing: Wynne Webber
Proofreading: Debra Hudson
Printing: Craft Print International Limited, Singapore
Film: Colour Chiefs, Brisbane
Acknowledgement: Holdfast Bay History Centre, Brighton, South Australia, for identifying the anchor of the *Trottman*, p. 22.

To view our extensive range of products, we invite you to visit the Steve Parish Publishing web site
www.steveparish.com.au

© copyright Steve Parish Publishing Pty Ltd, 2002
First published in Australia by Steve Parish Publishing Pty Ltd 2002
PO Box 1058, Archerfield, Queensland 4108, Australia
Email admin@steveparish.com.au

ISBN 1 74021 046 8

Produced in the Steve Parish Publishing studios, Australia.

Steve Parish
PUBLISHING